Marguerite, Misty and Me

The true story of a Newbery author, her celebrity pony and a fangirl turned history detective

Susan Friedland

Saddle Seeks Horse Press

Marguerite, Misty and Me

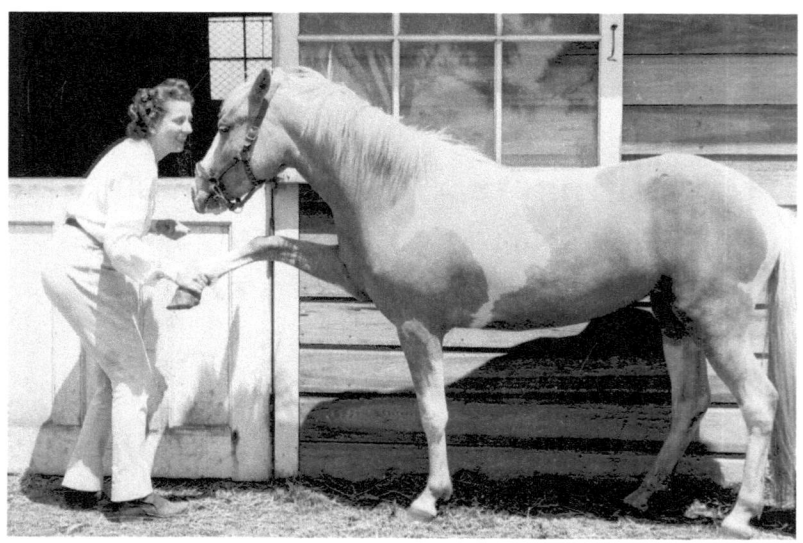

© 2024 Susan Friedland
Saddle Seeks Horse Press
All rights reserved.

Reproductions are with copyright permissions held by the University of Minnesota Libraries, Kerlan Collection of Children's Literature.

No part of this book may be reproduced in any form without written permission by the author, except in the case of brief quotations for articles, reviews or sharing on social media with attribution. The author encourages social media shares using the tag @saddleseekshorse.

Cover Design: Amy Summer Ellison
Back Cover Photo & Dedication Page Misty: NWJ Design & Photography
Photos of Susan and Knight: Carolyn Rikje
Illustrations: Bonnie Shields

Print Edition ISBN: 978-1-7327105-7-3
Ebook ISBN: 978-1-7327105-8-0
Hardcover ISBN: 978-1-7327105-9-7

Susan Friedland
saddleseekshorse.com

Dedication

For all my former English and history students—you were my teachers whether you realized it or not.
For every young person who has ever fallen in love with a book or an animal or both.
For my fellow horse fans—happy tales and trails!

Contents

Glossary	x
1. Wild, Swimming Ponies	1
2. The Horse Problem	5
3. Popular Pony Books	8
4. When Inspiration Strikes	14
5. The Idea Gallops Away with Me	20
6. The Newbery Medal and Other Awards	26
7. The Hands-off Horse	33
8. Marguerite from Milwaukee	36
9. Love in a Pine Forest	46
10. A Journalist's Journey	49
11. From Pretzel City to a Horse Community	53
12. The Real Misty Pony	58
13. Swimming with Horses	66
14. Marguerite's Writing Secrets	70

15.	Notes Everywhere	74
16.	The Struggle to Write Well	77
17.	Research and Cozy Details	84
18.	Traveling to the Setting	89
19.	Library Adventures	94
20.	Fan Letters and School Pictures	98
21.	Young Friends	106
22.	Influence Before Influencers Existed	112
23.	Chincoteague Pony Fun Facts	119
24.	Pony Penning Prelude	124
25.	Face to Face with Wild Ponies	128
26.	A Walk on the Beach	131
27.	Chincoteague Pony Superfans	135
28.	Games on Horseback	138
29.	The Pony Swim	143
30.	Bidding on a Foal	147
31.	The Swim Home	151
32.	A Website for a Pony	156
33.	A Pictorial Life Story of Misty	162
34.	Book Ideas and Unpublished Stories	168

35. Marguerite's Twilight	172
36. Marguerite's Kindness	178
37. Getting Lost While the Artwork Was Being Found	182
38. Marguerite, My Muse	187
Epilogue	194
Timeline of Marguerite Henry's Life	196
Interview with the Author	198
Notes	204
Image Credits	226
Acknowledgments	230
About the Author	232

Glossary

Archive—a place where old documents, photographs, and items of historical importance are stored, usually in a temperature and humidity-controlled room.

Assateague Island—a large wildlife refuge island off the coast of Maryland and Virginia, home to wild Chincoteague Ponies, sika deer, and over one hundred bird species.

Band—a family group of wild horses, consisting of a stallion with multiple mares and their foals.

Bay—a brown horse with a black mane and tail.

Burro—a donkey ("burro" is the Spanish word for donkey).

Chestnut—a reddish brown horse.

Chincoteague Island—the island between Assateague Island and the Virginia mainland. People live on Chincoteague and it has a long, history of chickens, oysters, folks from varied cultural backgrounds, and the Pony Penning Week Carnival.

Equestrian—a horseback rider.

Foal—a baby horse. A colt is a male foal and a filly is a female foal.

Ghostwriter—a skilled writer hired to write a book or article on behalf of another person.

Mare—an adult female horse. A filly will grow up to be a mare.

Newbery Medal—a prestigious award for children's literature. Think of it like the NBA's Most Valuable Player award or a singer winning a Grammy Award. Two of my favorites (besides *King of the Wind*) are *Maniac Magee* by Jerry Spinelli (1991) and *Bud, Not Buddy* by Christopher Paul Curtis (2000).

Pinto—a horse with large markings of color mixed with white. Misty was a palomino pinto (gold and white).

Primary source—a document, photo, newspaper article, diary or artifact, etc. that occurred at the time of the event. Marguerite used countless primary sources to research and write her stories, just as I used countless primary sources to write *Marguerite, Misty and Me*.

Saltwater Cowboys—firefighter-cowboys of the Chincoteague Volunteer Fire Company who oversee the Chincoteague Ponies on Assateague Island and round them up for the July pony swim.

Stallion—an adult male horse. In the wild, a colt will grow up to be a stallion and lead a band of mares.

Note: Each chapter of this book begins with a photo. If you want to know more about a particular photo, flip to the back of the book to the Image Credits section.

Chapter 1

Wild, Swimming Ponies

Murky clouds gave way to the sun, as a mass of cowboys on horseback and wet, wild ponies streamed toward me. Shouts of "Hey! Hey! Hey!" from the riders rang out as legions of legs sloshed through the Chincoteague Channel, off the coast of Virginia.

The Saltwater Cowboys, the riders on horseback, led the procession on a course that would take them just yards in front of my prime viewing spot—a rented tomato-red kayak. Stallions and mares with flowing manes and adorable, lanky foals followed them.

This was like having a front-row seat to the Kentucky Derby, but instead of awaiting the thunder of racehorses crossing the finish line, I awaited a wild pony swim, atop the water in the kayak.

Hundreds, maybe thousands, of other Chincoteague Pony fans of all ages were next to me and behind me in pontoon boats, fishing boats, canoes and rowboats. I even saw one person on a standup paddle board.

The crowd buzzed with excitement as watercraft "neighbors" struck up conversations. We had all gathered to watch the yearly crossing of around two hundred wild ponies. I was there on pony lookout because of my favorite childhood book, *Misty of Chincoteague* by Marguerite Henry. Have you ever loved a story from a book so much you wanted to live out the adventure?

When I was ten, I read *Misty* and fell in love with a young filly who swam with her herd from Assateague Island to nearby Chincoteague Island. Actually, Misty started the swim, but was so little, a whirlpool sucked her under the water. A boy named Paul Beebe, who was watching from a nearby boat, dove into the waves and swam alongside the foal, keeping her head afloat. Together they made it safely to the other side.

Paul and his sister Maureen had saved all their money and worked extra chores in order to buy this pony and her mom, the Phantom. Now I was there in person, decades later, to witness this real-life event I had read about repeatedly when I was a girl. My trip to Chincoteague Island, and this moment in the kayak, was the fulfillment of a lifelong dream.

The cowboys' horses and ponies coursed through the water, walking, walking, walking. A cluster of eager ponies, heads high, burst into a few strides of trot. Salt water sprayed.

"That one looks like Misty over there!" I said to myself, as a beautiful golden pony passed in front of me with a large white marking on its left side that resembled the shape of a map of the United States. The herd with the cowboys leading the way kept trudging through the channel.

For a second I thought, *Maybe this isn't really a swim, but just a walk through deep water, but a pony swim sounds more romantic for tourists.* Was it possible *Misty of Chincoteague* had overly dramatized this pony crossing? Disappointment loomed.

Suddenly, the lead cowboy's horse plunged chest-deep into the channel. Soon after, all the cowboys' horses dipped below the surface. Only their ears and noses peeked above the surf. My heart raced, and my kayak swayed.

Behind the Saltwater Cowboys, clusters of wild ponies began swimming too. I could only see the tops of their heads as they surged through the surf. "Yay, ponies!" I burst out. I videoed the splashing and paddling on my iPhone. The sun was so bright, I couldn't really tell what I was capturing. I was torn between watching the ponies swim in real time or preserving it to watch for months, maybe years to come.

A brown and white foal rested its chin on its mother's rump, catching a ride.

The ponies and cowboys grew smaller as they churned past. I craned my head left and watched them clamber up the shore and drop their heads to graze on the bright green marsh grasses. Hordes of fans snapped photos and pointed as the beautiful, wet herd munched and milled about.

Even though it lasted only a few minutes, the wild, swimming ponies were real, and their swim was better than how I imagined it from reading *Misty*. I couldn't wait to tell all my friends about the Chincoteague Ponies. The scene I witnessed was identical to the horse story from my childhood—the book whose words and pictures had seared into my heart, a story I will never forget.

Chapter 2

The Horse Problem

When I was a kid, I was obsessed with horses. I'm happy to report I never grew out of that obsession. But I had a huge problem—two problems, actually: my older sisters Linda and Renee. While I was experiencing horseless angst, my sisters were in college. This meant we couldn't afford any more large expenses. I begged my parents for a horse, but the answer was always no. Maybe you've begged your parents for something you yearn for and the answer is always "no." If so, I understand you.

Since I wasn't able to be with horses in real life, I spent as much time as I could reading about them. In the Dark Ages, before smartphones, apps and personal computers, I went to my local library.

At the Gail Borden Library, a brown brick building on the banks of the Fox River, I found stories with titles like *King of the Wind*, *Brighty of the Grand Canyon* and *Misty of Chincoteague*. These books by Marguerite Henry allowed me to adventure with horses in my imagination. Through Marguerite's words, I curried and cared for a shiny Arabian stallion in Morocco. Later, I navigated treacherous Grand Canyon pathways with a sure-footed little donkey (despite my fear of heights). But my favorite jaunt was galloping bareback on the Phantom, a black and white Chincoteague Pony (Misty's momma). That story whisked me away from my sunny yellow bedroom, decorated with pony posters and shelves lined with Breyer model horses, to an island in the Atlantic where Chincoteague Ponies scampered in freedom. While reading *Misty*, I could almost breathe in the saltwater aroma and hear the trumpet call of a stallion signaling to his band.

Then my life changed completely.

When I was around twelve, a friend of my parents invited me to ride! Cindy lived in the next town over, and soon I was spending time with her horses as often as possible. Her small herd lived in her backyard pastures, and those pastures connected with acres and acres of riding trails. Through her kindness, I graduated from loving horses in books to befriending them in person. I still didn't have a horse of my own, but I had access to borrowed horses, and that was a good place to start.

My regular ride was Jim Dandy—an experienced copper-colored Quarter Horse with white face that horse people refer to as "bald faced." I could ask Cindy's permission, then take Jim Dandy through the open spaces of Wayne, Illinois. Together, we pranced along the Prairie Path, trotted through twisty trails of a forest preserve, and wandered through fields fringed by cattails and white, lacy wildflowers. I've been smitten with horses ever since.

Somehow during those Wayne riding days, I learned my favorite author Marguerite Henry, the woman who wrote *Misty of Chincoteague*, had lived in this very village decades before I swung a leg over the saddle.

Riding the trails of Wayne was my happy place. Was it Marguerite's happy place too?

Chapter 3

Popular Pony Books

Like me, Marguerite Henry longed for a horse all her life. She never gave up on that dream and finally was able to buy her first horse when she was forty-four.

Her first horse, pony really, was Misty. The pretty pony with long blond eyelashes became the dream horse for me and many readers of *Misty of Chincoteague*. Rand McNally, a Chicago book publisher, released *Misty* in 1947. It later won the Newbery Honor (a prestigious award for children's literature—you have probably read a Newbery-winning book before—teachers love them), sold over a million copies, and was even made into a feature film released in 1961 by Twentieth Century Fox simply titled *Misty*.

When I first read *Misty*, I thought it was one hundred percent true. Later I learned that story and the two follow-up titles starring the golden pony are based on real people and real events, but some ideas and plot points came from Marguerite's imagination. Consider these next paragraphs as my book report summaries for *Misty*, *Sea Star* and *Stormy*, the books I lost myself in when I was your age.

The *Misty* story is set on a pony ranch near the islands of Chincoteague and Assateague, off the coast of Virginia, all places you can still visit today. Siblings Paul and Maureen Beebe lived there in the 1940s with their grandparents. The children long for a pony of their own. This is despite the fact that there are numerous ponies just outside their door and they assist Grandpa Beebe in gentling foals. They helped by training them so they could be sold as riding ponies. However, they want one special pony to love and keep forever.

Just like in real life, across the water from the pony ranch is an island with a red and white striped lighthouse with a backdrop of pine trees behind it. On Assateague Island, wild ponies believed to be descendants of Spanish shipwreck survivors frolic at the Atlantic's edge. The ponies are owned by the Chincoteague Volunteer Fire Company. Once a year, in

July during Pony Penning Week, horsemen go to Assateague to round up the bands of pintos, chestnuts, palominos, blacks and bays. The Saltwater Cowboys move the herd across a narrow channel to Chincoteague. And pony fans come out in droves to witness the swim.

In the story, Maureen and Paul have their hearts set on buying the Phantom, a clever pony who has always escaped the roundup. They keep their plan a secret from their grandparents and start saving money. Paul rides along with the roundup men on Assateague on the day of Pony Penning. He spots baby Misty struggling to swim next to her mother, the Phantom. As the foal's tiny head slips under the surf, the boy heroically leaps into the water and swims alongside the foal to keep her safe. The next day, the fire company holds a horse auction. There's a dramatic moment in *Misty of Chincoteague* when it appears the horses of Maureen and Paul's dreams will go home with another family. But then the other family wins a foal by raffle, so the Phantom and Misty join the Beebes.

Maureen and Paul train the Phantom. She becomes a riding horse and even wins a race, but Maureen notices she often leans out over the fence looking away toward the sea, toward Assateague. In contrast to her mother, Misty is curious and friendly, readily accepting the world of humans. In the end, the children release the Phantom back into the wild. They miss her, but they're grateful for Misty.

In real life, in order for Marguerite to write the forthcoming book, Misty came home with Marguerite. She needed to study pony behavior to write authentically about it. The pony lived in the Henrys' yard in Wayne, Illinois for about a decade.

Misty of Chincoteague is not the only book Marguerite would write based on real adventures of Chincoteague Ponies. The children who read Misty loved it so much, they begged Marguerite to write another book about the pony. At first, she had no intentions of penning such a story. Instead, she believed children could dream up their own wonderful sequels. However, a few years later, she learned a lone foal was found nuzzling its dead mother on Assateague. Marguerite sprang into action, composing the story *Sea Star: Orphan of Chincoteague*, a book she referred to as a postscript to *Misty*.

The plot of *Sea Star*, published in 1949, centers on movie producers offering to buy Misty so she can star in a film based on her life and tour around the country meeting children, many of whom had never seen or petted a pony in real life. Maureen and Paul are torn between dutifully accepting the offer, as it will help finance their uncle's college education, or keeping Misty for themselves. While the children consider the difficult decision, they stumble upon a bay orphan colt on the beach. They cleverly catch him by shooing him into the water and lifting him into their boat. They allow Misty to tour while they care for Sea Star.

The third book starring Misty is *Stormy, Misty's Foal*. This book was inspired by a dramatic, real-life event. In 1962, a deadly Nor'easter, a hurricane-like storm, pounded the Mid-Atlantic coast. Misty was living on the Beebe ranch at the time. At thirteen, she was pregnant with her third foal and about to give birth. Because of the flooding, a helicopter evacuated families to the mainland. Before the Beebes were evacuated, in order to keep Misty safe, they led Misty up the steps into their home and made an emergency stall out of their kitchen. They filled the sink with water like a trough. A mound of hay and a barn cat were her companions as she rode out the storm, unharmed, in the kitchen. The family's quick thinking and resourceful plan saved the celebrity pony. When the Beebes returned a few days later, Misty had opened the refrigerator and helped herself to the molasses jar. Soon after, she gave birth to a chestnut and white filly, aptly named Stormy.

Billy Beebe was the real-life grandson of Grandma and Grandpa Beebe and first cousin to Paul and Maureen. He was the owner of the Beebe Ranch before it was purchased by the Museum of Chincoteague. I visited the ranch once and Billy confirmed that all the Misty stories are based on true events. He once said the book *Misty* was seventy-five percent fiction and the book *Stormy, Misty's Foal* was twenty-five percent fiction. Regardless of the percentages, the beloved stories from my childhood felt true in my heart. If you haven't yet read *Misty of Chincoteague*, *Sea Star* and *Stormy, Misty's Foal*, I won't mind if you place your bookmark here, devour those other stories, and then come back to Chapter 4.

Chapter 4

When Inspiration Strikes

I thought it was amazing that some of my favorite horse stories were based on real events, but I didn't think much about Marguerite Henry and Misty for decades, until a few years ago. I was browsing through the bookshelf by my fireplace and found my ocean-blue hardcover copy of *Misty of*

Chincoteague and re-read it. The story took me not only to the the seashore, but back to my own childhood. And then I met a friend of a friend named Laura. Laura told me she had met Marguerite Henry many years earlier. Laura's story about my childhood hero made my heart leap.

"My mom and I had been fighting. I was ten and pretty much an ungrateful child. I wanted to go home. My mom said, 'No! I think you're going to like this. You see that lady right there? That's the one who writes your favorite books.' I was waiting in a long line under the shade of a eucalyptus tree with a very well-dressed woman sitting at a table. To me an author was a mythical creature ... I asked my mom what I was supposed to do. She said purchase her book. It was *Black Gold*. I got the book. 'Now walk up to her and tell her thank you.'

"I walked up I wasn't a shy kid, but I didn't understand the book signing thing. I introduced myself. She asked me what my favorite book was and if I had a horse. Her hair was swept up on her head in a little bun. She had this grace and style about her, and I was just mesmerized.

"She looked me right in the eyes. She was so sweet. I felt like I was really special to be there with that lady at that time. To this day, I love going to book signings. I just never forgot that experience—authors made these worlds for me. This probably happened in 1972, but I remember it like yesterday."

I did my best to imagine being at that book signing. I felt Marguerite's warmth and respect by the way she asked Laura about her horse status and favorite book. As beautiful and special as Marguerite's stories were, it seemed she was a beautiful and special woman whose story had never been told. Maybe I could be the one to tell it?

I did several online searches to try to find a biography of Marguerite Henry, but all I got were news articles and her obituary. My detective mode kicked in, and my curiosity about her life grew.

Perhaps I could research and discover the woman behind the books. It sounded like a fun activity and seemed like a way to make up for a bit of unfinished business I had. Let me explain.

When I was a teenager in the 1980s, I found out my mom's friend, Mary Ellen, had ridden the pony Misty when she was a little girl. I couldn't believe it!

My mom told Mary Ellen how much I adored Marguerite and her book *Misty*, and Mary Ellen gave my mom a black-and-white photograph. It showed a little girl wearing a cowboy hat and a smug smile sitting aboard a palomino pinto. It was Mary Ellen when she was young, riding Misty! She also gave me Marguerite Henry's California address. My mom framed the snapshot of Misty and Mary Ellen, and I held on to Marguerite's address.

The cream page with blue cursive words bearing my favorite author's exact location overwhelmed me. I couldn't believe I now possessed a link to someone so famous and respected! I longed to know and, probably without realizing it, be known by Mrs. Henry. But as a shy girl with perfectionistic tendencies, I placed the treasure in my desk. Maybe one day I'd know what to say to my hero. That day never came. Marguerite died at the age of ninety-five in 1997. The paper with the Rancho Santa Fe P.O. Box number remained filed and out of sight, my fan letter unwritten.

If Laura had such vivid memories of the author, surely I could find other people willing to share their memories of her too. Maybe I would gather enough information to write an article or two for a horse magazine.

I was a seventh grade teacher living in Los Angeles at the time, but I went to visit my mom in Illinois over spring break. Together, we visited her friend from long ago—Mary Ellen. We stepped into her room at the assisted living center, and she greeted us with smiles and hugs. I showed her the framed picture of her aboard Misty of Chincoteague, and her face softened. I asked her about the pony, but she was unable to answer my questions. She remembered her cowgirl outfit and how she met Marguerite through her grandmother's librarian friend, Mildred Lathrop. Later, I showed her pictures of my bay Thoroughbred gelding Knight, and she said he was beautiful. Even though I hadn't learned much about Misty, I was glad to make Mary Ellen smile.

Our next stop was the police station in the village of Wayne. I introduced myself to the officers, mentioning I learned to ride in nearby fields and across the street at the riding school. I asked them if they could help me find anyone who would remember Marguerite. While one officer made a couple of phone calls, a man entered the station and started up a conversation with another officer. I recognized his voice immediately.

He was Cindy's son—the woman who had let me ride Jim Dandy and given me an entry point to the horse world in real life, just as Marguerite had given me entry through the pages of her stories. We laughed and tried to remember the last time we had seen each other. He told me I hadn't changed a bit in the past forty years, which I knew wasn't true since I no longer wore purple eyeshadow nor permed my hair. I asked how his mom was doing and learned she had passed away several years prior. I said I was sorry. Cindy had been such a spirited person; she loved to ride at a gallop.

Later, I reflected on how no one would have the chance to get to know Cindy anymore. It was the same with Marguerite. I thought of my unwritten fan letter and felt a sense of urgency. I had to find out what I could about Marguerite from the people who knew her, before they, like Cindy, no longer blazed about in the saddle.

Chapter 5

The Idea Gallops Away with Me

Around this same time I heard Laura's story of meeting Marguerite, I took up the equestrian sport of foxhunting, and it made me think of Marguerite again.

In California, where I was living at the time, the term "foxhunting" is not totally accurate. "Coyote chasing" is a better description. Hunt club members ride their horses at cattle ranches serving as seasonal territory guardians. By riding through cattle pastures, the horses and hounds keep coyotes at bay so cows can deliver their calves in peace.

I met Creole Rose, a red Thoroughbred, sporting a braided mane and a snaffle bridle. I had rented this mare to ride in my first foxhunt on a ranch that had been used as a location for filming westerns. Rugged mountain peaks edged the skyline and sagebrush danced along the ground. Mahogany brown cows grazed in the distance. The Master of Foxhounds, a horseman and leader of the hunt club, arranged for me to ride the mare. He said Rose's owner was a woman in her seventies, and that both little kids and people who were out of shape had foxhunted on her. He promised me that by the end of my ride, I would not want to leave the saddle because Rose was the best.

I mounted and patted Rose's neck, trying both to form a bond and quiet my nerves.

The fieldmaster, our mounted guide, led our group of a dozen riders down a dusty lane at the walk as we watched the hunting staff in their scarlet coats and the wagging tails of the hounds, eagerly sniffing and scampering, hundreds of yards ahead of us.

Our group picked up the pace and trotted. Rose's forward stride caused me to rise and fall in the saddle at quick, comical intervals of a rising trot. A few of the horses began cantering along, so Rose opened up her stride into a canter, and I hovered over the saddle like a jockey. I rode the waves of her gait as the meadow narrowed into a shaded grove of pines. Rose was so fast, I wasn't sure how I could slow her down since she kept ignoring my hands squeezing the reins, telling her "whoa." I worried she would slam into the backsides of the horses just a few feet ahead of us. But Rose knew her job. When the horses slowed, she automatically did too.

Under the canopy of trees, on a carpet of rust-colored pine needles, horses and riders paused to catch their breath. We took turns maneuvering our mounts in groups of twos and threes over to the water trough for refreshment. Two sandy colored hounds leaped into the trough for a quick cool off in between horses' slurping. The fieldmaster asked our group if we were doing okay. I was doing more than okay. I loved every minute of this riding adventure!

If you have never ridden a horse, I can't recommend it enough. In fact, you might want to pause for a minute, find your nearest parent and ask them to arrange for you to go ride a horse. You can thank me later.

Back when I was a kid, I had ridden Jim Dandy in a foxhunt once in Wayne, Illinois, as Cindy's guest. I was twelve. That hunt club was just down the road on the other side of the street from where Marguerite Henry lived. I wondered if

Marguerite had ever foxhunted. I decided that the next time I traveled back to Illinois to visit my family I could investigate by talking to someone from the Illinois hunt club.

Following our water break, we picked up the pace again. As we were cantering along, I realized a ditch sprawled on the path ahead of us. It wasn't a giant chasm, but a ditch nonetheless. I had never jumped a ditch before, but we were moving so fast I didn't have time to think or even get scared. Rose sprinted, and for a split second, soared. I giggled and declared, "I just jumped a ditch!" My eyes were wet, either from the wind in my face or the exhilaration, maybe both.

After the ditch, a short, steep hill, strewn with large rocks, lurked ahead of us. It looked impassable. Before I knew it, the whole group, including Rose and me, trotted and cantered up the hill. I would have *never* considered going up that hill if I were out on a trail ride with my horse Knight. I didn't see a path; it looked impassable. These hunt horses navigated like mountain goats. I exclaimed, "I can't believe we just went up that hill!" I'm sure some of the seasoned women I rode alongside were smiling at my newbie commentary.

Then we galloped. I couldn't remember the last time I had experienced the freedom of a gallop. It had been years.

At the end of the ride when I reached the horse trailer and removed the saddle from Rose, now covered in sweat, I shared with horseman how I laughed and cried and had a blast, thanking him for making it all possible. He replied, "This is the most fun a person will ever have on horseback."

As I reflected on the thrill of that ride during my two-hour drive back to my suburban home, I realized why that riding adventure made my heart sing: This is how I learned to ride as a kid! Aboard another red horse named Jim Dandy, I flew through fields and forests and experienced a freedom and joy I still crave. That was the day I fell in love with this friendship-forming, non-competitive, hours-in-nature way of riding called foxhunting. I was hooked.

John Muir, the naturalist, once observed, "Between every two pines is a doorway to a new world." Astride a red mare, between rustling pines on a cattle ranch in the mountains, I found a new world, and it was remarkably like that of my youth. Those galloping hoofbeats I first encountered on the pages of *Misty* thundered beneath me in real life.

***

Next, I began searching for information on Marguerite at Gail Borden Library in Elgin, Illinois—the library of my youth. I was exhilarated to discover *my* library was the same library where Marguerite researched for her books. For example, her librarian friend Mildred Lathrop, who had also introduced her to Mary Ellen, showed her a *Sunset* article titled "Brighty, Free Citizen" about a little burro who lived in the Grand Canyon and was the first brave soul to cross the suspension bridge built across Bright Angel Creek. Marguerite's story of that donkey was published in 1953 as *Brighty of the Grand Canyon,* and you can read about the harrowing creek crossing in the chapter titled "Well Done!"

I approached a librarian named Phyllis to ask for help.

"I'm here to look up information in local newspapers on the children's author Marguerite Henry. She used to live near here a long time ago."

A wide smile spread across her face. "When I was in elementary school, I wrote Marguerite Henry a letter and she wrote me back. I still have it somewhere."

It was a great start to my search, and soon I was finding connections everywhere. I grew to know Marguerite each time I read one of her out-of-print books and every time I talked with someone at a historical society or library. With each tidbit of information I gained about the people, places and practices that influenced Marguerite, I was more and more inspired to share her story with the world. I wanted to remember Marguerite and Misty, and I wanted to introduce them both to readers who had not yet met the author and her pretty pony.

Chapter 6

The Newbery Medal and Other Awards

One day while I was on my laptop researching Marguerite, I found an online article mentioning an archival collection of Marguerite Henry papers. I reread the sentence. My mind raced. I did some more Googling and discovered that a library at the University of Minnesota had thirty-six boxes filled with personal documents and artifacts of Marguerite Henry. The boxes were categorized by the titles of her books. Some boxes contained fan letters, some contained awards, and some contained unpublished manuscripts. This finding was better than a buried treasure of gold. Off to Minnesota, Land of Ten Thousand Lakes, I went.

At the research library, I had to put all my belongings in a locker except for a pencil, a notebook, my laptop and my iPhone, before I could go in to view the boxes. I was thrilled when I reached the box containing Marguerite's Newbery Award! This prestigious award was created in 1922 to honor and encourage quality books for children. Before this award, children's books were rarely read by adults, and many considered them unimportant compared to books for adults. *King of the Wind* won the John Newbery Award in 1949. *Justin Morgan Had a Horse*, Marguerite's first horse book, and *Misty of Chincoteague* won Newbery Honors, as runners up in 1946 and 1948 respectively.

Marguerite's Newbery Medal rests in a black felt frame about the size of a square coaster. One side of the medal reads, "For the most distinguished contribution to American literature for children." Marguerite's name and the year are engraved onto an open book with a torch blazing behind it. A laurel wreath encircles the torch. I held Marguerite's prize in my hand, thinking about and wondered what it meant to her. Where did she keep it at her house?

When I picked up *King of the Wind* as a girl, I didn't realize it was an award-winning book; I just wanted to read more horse stories. In its pages I was swept away across centuries. I journeyed with Agba, the mute stable boy who saved the sultan's orphan foal with love and camel's milk. When Sham matured into a stunning stallion, he was gifted to King Louis XV of France, and I imagined voyaging across the Mediterranean with the boy and the horse. My spirit drooped when Sham emerged from the ship so undernourished that the king rejected him. He was sold as a cart horse. I felt like I was there every step of the way as the horse and his devoted friend endured hardship, separation, reunion, exile, then redemption.

King of the Wind introduced me to people from another culture. I didn't understand the Ramadan fasting or the call to prayer in the opening scene of the story, but I understood Agba's devotion to a horse. The boy on the other side of the world living in another era, practicing a different religion, wasn't so different from me. Marguerite opened my eyes to the world beyond my small town.

Back in the 1940s, Marguerite was invited to a press conference where Frederic Melcher announced the winners of the Newbery Award. Despite a blustery snowstorm, reporters and photographers came out in force. Wesley Dennis, Marguerite's illustrator, came as a surprise guest. *Publisher's Weekly* reported, "The more you know about the author of the prize-winning book, *King of the Wind* (Rand McNally), the more certain you become that no accolade has ever been more judiciously presented. You'll never learn from Marguerite herself about this highest of honors in the juvenile field that she has won. Would that the great in all avenues of creative accomplishment were as modest as Marguerite Henry!"

Mary Alice Jones, Marguerite's editor, repeated how Marguerite was never one to brag: "It is a delight to work with her on a manuscript. She is so eager for suggestions, so delighted with the smallest contribution in the way of an idea or phrase that she makes one feel her own joy in creating the material. And when it's finally completed and published and offered to the public, she seems to have a continual feeling of surprised pleasure that people really like it well enough to buy it."

People didn't just like *King of the Wind*, they loved it. Marguerite received a flurry of invitations to schools, book fairs, horse shows and libraries. And Marguerite wasn't the only one invited. "One day the world in all its bigness opened out for Misty with a formal invitation to her from the American Library Association. She sniffed it indifferently while I read in disbelief." Author and pony traveled to the convention in Michigan, where a stall was prepared for Misty in the auditorium exhibit hall.

Once in the host city, Misty attended an early morning meeting of librarians. A photo in *A Pictorial Life Story of Misty* shows the mare amid several seated rows of well-dressed librarians. Misty's muzzle is at Marguerite's shoulder. A straight-faced woman in a feathered hat sits behind the pony's rump. A nearby woman wearing a horse pin on her lapel grins.

Misty was not invited to come to dinner and the acceptance speech, but she did get to go to a party before the banquet. According to Marguerite, the pony leaped into the hotel elevator and traveled to the seventh floor where she hobnobbed with important people in the publishing world. The dignitaries gave her carrots. Not everyone was thrilled to have a live horse at the conference, but it made a great news story.

At the dinner, Marguerite spoke about her writing experience: "*King of the Wind* was a long time growing. At first it was nothing but a letterhead. A letterhead and a wish." She concluded her speech, "Sometimes a book gives you a small moment of happiness; and sometimes when you close the cover, the book grows big within you, like a boll of cotton bursting its seams … if it weren't for deadlines I'd still be working on *King of the Wind*. The doing is always so much more fun than the getting through … Now this book is finished. Sham has been crowned, and in the crowning Agba too has been honored. As custodian for them I accept the Newbery Medal."

After the ceremony, Misty visited the banquet hall to have her photo taken by *The Grand Rapids Press* newspaper. She stood between rows of tables, chairs were askew. Before the author and pony left Grand Rapids, they had an autograph party at Herpolsheimer's department store. Book display counters were removed "to provide space for a stall for Marguerite Henry's little island horse, Misty, which proved, over a two-hour period, to be a perfect guest." During the pony party, Marguerite signed books by the hundreds and Misty delighted "hordes of children who crowded the store."

Marguerite had won several awards before receiving her Newbery Medal. Her sister Gertrude proudly listed them in a magazine article she wrote about her little sister: "Three of her books had been Junior Literary Guild selections: *The Little Fellow, Justin Morgan Had a Horse*, and *Misty of Chincoteague*. *Justin Morgan* received the 'Friends of Literature' Award for 1946. *Benjamin West and His Cat, Grimalkin* was listed by the Library of Congress among juvenile books of 1947 best expressing the American spirit. It has been translated into two foreign languages and done into Braille, as has also *King of the Wind*. *The Little Fellow* has just gone into a Spanish edition."

Gertrude then wrote, "Just as highly treasured as these recognitions, however, are the letters which come to Marguerite Henry from boys and girls. Honors and awards are sobering, almost frightening to her, and there is little danger that they will ever go to her head."

Chapter 7

The Hands-off Horse

There seemed to be no shortage of sources to learn about the famous author Marguerite Henry, but I began wondering what her childhood was like. After learning some basic information, I was inspired to play detective and unearth clues about the early years of my favorite author.

Marguerite was born in Milwaukee in 1902 to Louis and Anna Breithaupt. I found that out from Wikipedia. That was the same year my Grandpa Friedland was born. She was a Midwesterner, just like me. Cool.

A *Chicago Tribune* article revealed that when she was a girl, Marguerite's family owned a mare named Bonnie. However, things were complicated with the family steed. "I wasn't allowed anything to do with it. She was Bonnie by name and in appearance, but not in disposition. She had a habit of biting my brother in the breeches and leaving big teeth marks. Besides being a nipper, Bonnie was also a bucker and a bolter."

Her protective brother Fred was fifteen years older than her and didn't allow Marguerite to ride. In fact, he never even allowed her to touch their horse. That seemed extreme. Marguerite remembered her brother fondly. He would pick her up and twirl her, so she flew through the air. Yet she wanted to fly on the back of a horse. She dreamed of riding.

When she was much older, Marguerite wrote to a school district describing her love of all animals. She wrote about playing with her animals when she was a little girl, loving them so much she believed they would grow up and be able to talk. Placing them on her pillow, she would shut her bedroom door and go away for an hour, thinking upon her return, they would be able to speak "small words in a small voice." She didn't specify if they were real pets or stuffed animals, but it seems unlikely they were alive. The only childhood pet I could find evidence of was a guinea pig, and that animal surely would not have remained on Marguerite's pillow.

Even though her childhood animals never spoke, the stories she wrote gave voices to horses, dogs, cats, foxes and a burro. Decades later, these characters speak to readers not in small words, in small voices, but in expressions and actions so memorable, the characters are almost impossible to forget.

My own childhood, spent longing for a horse I wouldn't get until I was a teenager, felt similar to Marguerite's. I admired the way she held onto her dream. Although she wouldn't be able to enjoy a horse of her own until she was in her forties, Marguerite took up her pen to bring the joy of horses into the world.

My local library in Elgin had given up its secrets. It was time to set off for Milwaukee, where I hoped to find the home where Marguerite grew up, her schools, where she hung out as a kid, and perhaps some surprising details about her life. I couldn't wait to get to know my favorite author better through archival research. I hoped I would get to know her well enough that I could introduce her to all my friends, and learn from her example. And although I was an adult, I wanted to grow up to be just like her.

Chapter 8

Marguerite from Milwaukee

I continued my research at the Milwaukee County Historical Society. Marble columns, dazzling chandeliers and ornate gold designs along the high ceilings made me feel like I had entered a castle, not an archive that had once been a bank.

I already knew Louis and Anna Breithaupt welcomed their fifth and final child, Marguerite Anna, into the world on April 13, 1902. I'd found a few other details about her childhood as I scoured libraries and the internet, but I was hoping to find an old map or photographs or historical records. I was optimistic the historical archive held hidden clues about my favorite author.

Marguerite painted a happy picture of her childhood in *Junior Book of Authors*. "We lived in a modest little home in Milwaukee and no youngster had a happier period of growing up. Marie, my oldest sister, made my dresses, embroidered and sashed in blue, and gave me music lessons. Elsie, a young nurse, taught me the doorknob method of pulling teeth and provided an allowance which was all the more exciting because of its irregularity. Fred, my big brother, used to take my hand and run with me, so that I flew through space in the most astounding manner, like a creature who could glide without wings."

Gertrude, who was five years older than Marguerite, was her personal dictionary. While reading *Little Women* as a young girl, Marguerite read the word "gingerly." She asked Gertrude what it meant. Off the top of her head, Gertrude brought the word to life: "Papa has a drippy head cold, and this morning when he accidentally dropped his handkerchief, you picked it up very gingerly." As an adult, Marguerite turned to Gertrude for input on her books, stating, "Editors could be wrong, but not Gertrude."

Marguerite inherited her love for words from her father Louis Breithaupt, a man who recited poetry and Shakespeare and yodeled around the house. Louis was the president and owner of L. Breithaupt Printing Co. On rainy Saturdays, Marguerite joined her father at the print shop. The whirring presses and printed materials fascinated the future author. She pretended to read proofs from her father's office, stating, "It was then, I think, the printer's ink got into my blood."

During the holidays, the Breithaupt family presented poems and staged original plays they had written for each other. The Christmas she was seven, Marguerite received a gift unusual for a young girl in the early 1900s: a writer's desk, a small red table outfitted with tools for an aspiring writer. Supplies included a cream pitcher containing sharpened pencils, scissors tied with string to the table, paste, paper clips, a pencil sharpener, and a mound of colorful paper from her father's office. Her father had written on the top sheet,

> "Dear Last of the Mohicans, Not a penny for your thoughts, but a tablet. Merry Christmas! Papa Louie xoxo"

The last o contained a doodled smiley face.

Young Marguerite's desk was tucked into a cozy corner of the kitchen. While her mother and the family's German cook meal prepped, Marguerite played with words. "While I scribbled and sketched at the little red table I was supremely happy. All about me were the most titillating smells and sounds—an egg whisk beating against its bowl, soups and sauces purring and boiling, the clink of clean knives and forks being dropped into their trays, and Mama and the hired girl chatting away about things that didn't matter to me. But what did matter to me was that they were there, and they were working too."

Marguerite later purchased pushpins with her allowance so she could secure her "precious gems" on her desk. The following quotes were once attached to her writing space:

Next to mother's milk, books are the best nourishment. —Lawrence Clark Powell

The more you read, the better you write. —Anonymous

Marguerite's mother Anna enjoyed reading *The Delineator*. This magazine was published by Butterick, the pattern company, and featured articles on fashion, culture and fine arts. The magazine burst with serial adventure stories and there was even a column titled "Sewing School for Children."

When *The Delineator* held a writing contest for children, Marguerite entered. She wrote "Hide and Seek in Autumn Leaves," based on a game at a friend's birthday party. Marguerite had buried herself under a mound of crispy leaves, sure no one would find her. If it hadn't been for the birthday girl giving her dog one of Marguerite's gloves to sniff, Marguerite might have missed out on the party. Her hiding spot was that good. The hound sniffed her out just in time for cake and hot chocolate. Marguerite wrote that the cake's frosting was so thick, she wished she had the dog's long tongue to lap it up.

The Breithaupt family rejoiced when Marguerite's story won the contest and was published. She received $12 for her work, valued around $350 today. In a note of congratulations, the editor suggested Marguerite should use the money to attend summer camp. The budding tween writer took this suggestion and registered for a church camp on Lake Pistakee in northern Illinois. I tried to locate "Hide and Seek in Autumn Leaves," Marguerite's first published article, poring over issue after issue of *The Delineator*, pausing to read ads for soap and Victrolas. I was unable to find it.

However, I was successful in finding Lake Pistakee, which is about an hour from my home. A local historian, my mom and I enjoyed lunch under an umbrella overlooking the shimmery water where over one hundred years ago, Marguerite splashed with her cabinmates.

Marguerite's Sunday school teacher, Laura Bertelson, doubled as camp counselor in charge of the gaggle of girls. One night around a campfire, she asked her charges their favorite hobbies. As Marguerite's fellow campers burst out with swimming, tennis and skiing, the young writer felt awkward, realizing all those hobbies were active pursuits.

With a dry throat she stuttered, "My hobby is words." Her shy announcement was met with momentary silence. Then as she was wishing to "'throw myself on the fire and turn to ash dust,' Miss Bertelson said, 'What a coincidence! I like to play with words, too. What kind do you like, Marguerite?'"

Marguerite recalled, "It was too late now to become popular. I slid deeper into a quagmire of my misery as I confessed, 'tin-tin-nabulation.'" Laura acknowledged Marguerite's appreciation for *The Bells* by poet Edgar Allan Poe, smoothing out an awkward moment for the young word lover.

It's possible Marguerite was not into outdoor sports because of the rheumatic fever she had from ages ten to twelve. Marguerite stayed home from school for an extended amount of time because of the illness. During what could have been a lonely and boring chapter of life, she turned to books.

Young Marguerite enjoyed at least one physical activity: roller skating. When she was healthy, she made a habit of skating one mile every other day to Milwaukee's North Side Branch Library to check out a new book and return the one she had just finished reading.

One day, as Marguerite roller skated to the library to return *Hans Brinker*, a Dutch tale about an aspiring speed skater, a motorcycle nearly hit her. In order to avoid a collision, the driver thrust out an arm. He successfully shoved Marguerite out of the way, but she and the book fell down hard. Marguerite's concern was not for her own scrapes and bruises, but for the precious book. She thought of the ominous signs at the library about how defaced books would result in the borrower losing library privileges. For a bibliophile, a lover of books, that was an unimaginable fate!

As an adult, Marguerite reflected, "What greater punishment could there be than to forgo a new book every other day? From the viewpoint of my scant years it would be far worse than a 'no vacancy' sign on the gates of heaven."

Marguerite, now wearing a head bandage, at last brought the scraped-up book to a librarian. Miss Orvitz took her by the hand and led her to a glorious backroom—a book hospital. Together, they repaired *Hans Brinker*, and Marguerite enjoyed the task. In fact, Miss Ovitz later hired Marguerite to work at the library after school and on Saturdays as an official book mender!

I wanted to retrace Marguerite's roller skating route, so I got help from an archivist at the Milwaukee County Historical Society. First, he showed me the Polk City Directory, a thin-paged precursor to a telephone book. In the wide-spined yet delicate century-old book, I found Marguerite's childhood street address and an advertisement for L. Breithaupt

Printing Co.: "Our printing is planned to attract and convince."

I chuckled when the archivist approached my table cradling the largest book I had ever seen, a Sanborn Fire Insurance Map. It looked like a movie prop. He opened the massive book—it spanned about four feet across the table—and flipped through pages, eventually landing on the lot location of Marguerite's childhood home. He said that it was still a residential neighborhood and chances were good the house was still there. Later that afternoon, I drove around the neighborhood. To my dismay, instead of Marguerite's house, I found an empty driveway. The Breithaupt home had been demolished and paved to make parking spots for a leaning Victorian house next door.

Once the archivist and I had found the location of the Breithaupt home, we began searching for the North Side Branch Library where Marguerite had skated and worked. Although the building is long gone, we found a photograph that showed the library had once been in the same building as a natatorium—a public swimming pool. That cracked me up. Books and a dip, anyone?

With a flash of curiosity, I asked the curator if they had any high school yearbooks from the early 1900s. He disappeared for several minutes, returning with four Riverside University High School yearbooks from 1917-1920. Eager to see pictures of Marguerite as a teenager, I began searching the Bs for Breithaupt.

I found the teenage Marguerite with wide eyes and dark wavy bobbed hair. Her name and photos were peppered throughout the yearbooks, as she was active in several student organizations like the drama club and a camaraderie club. Her senior class picture lists her name and her nickname "Breity." *Was this where she came up with the name for Brighty the burro in her book Brighty of the Grand Canyon?*

Not surprisingly, Marguerite was also on the yearbook staff and wrote three pages of a fantastical class prophecy in *The Mercury*. I read later that she was also sending romance stories to *The Atlantic*, but they were never published.

Even though she was active in school and seemingly not shy, Marguerite once wrote that she was very thin and wore multiple layers of socks to school so no one would notice her skinny legs.

After admiring the Art Deco fonts and designs of the yearbooks, I thought about the world events that happened during Marguerite's high school years: World War I raged and ended, the Spanish Flu swept through the country, prompting debate on vaccines, and in 1920, the year she graduated, women got the right to vote with the passing of the 19th Amendment.

The archivist helped me track down Marguerite's college records as well. She attended a college that is today the University of Wisconsin-Milwaukee. She was a journalism student and member of multiple clubs. She served as vice-president of the Dramatic Club and was a member of the the French Club, a literary club, and the English Club—a selective campus club only open to students with "special ability in literary appreciation and composition, as determined by the English faculty."

Again Marguerite wrote for the yearbook. An excerpt from her poem titled "Femininity," published in *The Echo*, made me think of a flapper, perhaps a woman she tried to be like, and reveals her skill for description.

I mark the brilliant color of her cheek,
The pretty, tilted snub of powdered nose,
The childish treble voice, so soft and meek,
The silken swish of super-stylish clothes.

Marguerite's college career ended well when she performed in a play titled *The World and His Wife*, based on a 1920s romance film. Records don't show whether Marguerite had a lead role, but she wrote that she couldn't have her parents attend and see her smoking a fake cigarette.

Shortly after graduation, Marguerite got swept up in her own romance, one that lasted a lifetime.

Chapter 9

Love in a Pine Forest

In 1922, the summer after graduating from college, Marguerite joined her sister Gertrude and brother-in-law Russell on vacation. They stayed at Huber's Woodland Resort on Lake Minocqua in Wisconsin's Northwoods. It was an area popular for golf courses, boating and beaches with clean white sand. I've heard old tales of fishers catching muskies over five feet long from the crystal clear waters. The region continues to lure outdoor lovers to its pine forest paradise.

It's not clear how Sidney Henry, a hazel-eyed traveling salesman living in Chicago, crossed paths with the lanky word lover from Milwaukee, but the pair had an instant connection. They fished together by day and at night danced to a pianist's plinking keys on a piano Marguerite described as in need of a good tuning.

David R. Collins, in his book *Write a Book for Me: The Story of Marguerite Henry*, described Sidney as a "tall and slender ... bespectacled young businessman [who] was clearly well read, with opinions based on fact gathering. He attracted Marguerite's attention upon their first meeting. They spent the afternoons fishing and sharing their thoughts and even their future dreams."

On their way home, the Breithaupt sisters stopped by Sidney's parents' home in Sheboygan, close to the shore of Lake Michigan. The Henrys' vegetable garden was at its peak, and the group had lunch, including home grown sweet corn and juicy tomatoes. As they said goodbye, they agreed to meet again the next summer.

But Sidney couldn't wait. He arrived at the Breithaupt home a few weeks later to meet Marguerite's parents. His visit must have been positive, although her mother warned Marguerite that once a traveler, always a traveler.

Not long after, the young lovers' engagement announcement appeared in *The Milwaukee Journal*, with a photograph of Marguerite. She looks like a fashionable flapper wearing a sparkling headband with a long feather. She is posed in a profile view, in the center of two other brides-to-be.

Marguerite and Sidney married on Saturday, May 5, 1923. *The Sheboygan Press-Telegram*, Sidney's hometown newspaper, recorded the ceremony in vivid detail with emphasis on the clothing. I'm convinced the bride herself was the author.

"The bride's gown was of white georgette crepe with panels of beaded crystal and a girdle of braided silver. Her tulle veil fell from a coronet of pearls and crystals and she carried a shower bouquet of lilies of the valley, white sweetpeas and sweetheart roses."

They had a luxurious reception at the Hotel Astor in downtown Milwaukee, under a vibrant stained glass dome and glistening chandeliers. The Astor stands today, but it is now an apartment building.

You might be thinking romance would get in the way of Marguerite's career in journalism, but it actually had the opposite effect.

Chapter 10

A Journalist's Journey

A mishap with her wedding gifts propelled Marguerite's professional writing career. In a 1968 interview with the *Chicago Tribune*, Marguerite said she and Sidney "received five lamps, so I bought five tables. I didn't want to hurt anyone's feelings by returning the gifts. Instead, it was my husband who was hurt and shocked by my extravagance. The only way I could make amends, I thought, was to pay for the tables myself. I had to have a job. Quickly. But all I could do was write."

The next day, the newlywed walked into a magazine publishing office and asked for an assignment. She told the editor if her writing was not acceptable, he would not have to pay her. The bold plan worked. On July 7, 1924, Marguerite, then twenty-two, soon found herself squished in a crowd in front of one of the tallest buildings of that time. She did her best to listen to the dedication for an expensive new skyscraper, the American Furniture Mart. Unfortunately, she did not manage to write enough notes for a complete article.

The aspiring journalist didn't want her first assignment to be her last, so after the ceremony, the aspiring reporter shoved her way through the crowd to the speaker.

"'Governor Morrow,' I gasped, 'this is my very first assignment and I can't remember half the things you said. If you'd only repeat the high spots so I could take notes!'" The governor handed her a copy of his whole speech. Marguerite wrote the story, realizing, "All I had to do was boil it down. And that was fun. I've been boiling things down ever since."

The next year, Marguerite wrote a series of articles for *Photoplay* magazine's interior decorating column. I wonder if "Ornamental Lamps, Well Placed Add Beauty and Restfulness" was inspired by her honeymoon lamp squabble with Sidney. I would love to know if her husband read this article and if so, what his reaction was.

Eventually, Marguerite began ghostwriting for business magazines. She even contributed to World Book Encyclopedia. Marguerite did so much ghostwriting, she wrote an article in 1935 for *Writer's Digest* magazine titled "Adventures of a Ghost Writer." The essay shares Marguerite's methods. She asserts, "One thing that writing on assignment teaches you is that you can write any time, anywhere. And you don't have to be in a certain mood."

For instance, once Marguerite was on the fifteenth floor of a hotel in St. Louis during a power outage because of a tornado. She had to walk down and up the stairs for a meal since room service wasn't working. Meanwhile, she was composing an article on grandfather clocks. When her usually harsh editor received the article, he declared, "The grandfather clock piece was the most vivid thing you've ever done. Every one of your verbs conveyed action."

As a sales manager, Sidney's job required him to crisscross the country, frequently staying in one large city or another for a month at a time, and Marguerite went with him. She liked to try to get magazine articles published wherever they were staying. Once during a stint in Philadelphia, Marguerite read a list of local publishers to Sidney. When she said the words "Saturday Evening Post," Sidney encouraged Marguerite to try it. At first Marguerite was shocked. The magazine was very well known. Then she thought, "Why not?" After all, the worst they could say was no, and she had heard nos before.

"To Sid's lack of surprise and my disbelief, the Post bought a three-part series from me 'Turning Points in the Lives of Famous Men.'" The series featured Clarence Darrow. When they met, the famed Chicago attorney grilled the young journalist as though he were the one conducting the interview.

Through writing, the future children's book author met many important people of her time. But Marguerite wasn't as interested in working with famous people and leaders of industry as she was in writing children's stories. Years later, a child asked Marguerite why her books were always about animals, and she said, "I feel so comfortable with them. They never complain, never gossip, never go on strike … Brighty [her donkey] and Misty have become celebrities, but do they want a yacht or a castle? No. A pail of water, a measure of oats, and a loving hand are all they ask. I guess the answer is simple. I like animals."

Chapter 11

From Pretzel City to a Horse Community

In 1933, the Henrys left the bustling city of Chicago and began their lives in a farm town. This is where Marguerite's career as an author began. They moved to a white cottage by a river in "Pretzel City" Freeport, Illinois. Mr. Twist the pretzel is the Freeport High School mascot today, a nod toward the town's German roots. Freeport is where Marguerite met some of the people who would inspire her early stories as well as an illustrator who lived nearby.

Gladys Rourke Blackwood, a woman who lived near Marguerite in Freeport, studied at the Art Institute of Chicago. During the 1930s, she had a gallery in Chicago, and she became well-known for her paper doll designs, some of which sell for a lot today, and her greeting card and wrapping paper designs. She had been born with a birth defect and could only use one of her hands, but she used her hand well, creating art that delighted Marguerite.

When they arrived in Freeport, the Henrys hired Effendi and Beda Walkeala to be their handyman and cook. As Beda baked bread in the kitchen and Effendi whittled small flowers out of blocks of wood, the duo shared stories of growing up in Finland. Marguerite listened intently and was inspired to write a short story based on one tale. Marguerite published her first book, *Auno and Tauno: a Story of Finland*, illustrated by her neighborhood friend Blackwood in 1940. It tells of twins Auno and Tauno skiing to school, gliding past reindeer while carrying herring in their lunch bags. The family's gray horse, Tapio, pulls them in a sleigh under the northern lights. The book sold for one dollar.

According to Marguerite's older sister Gertrude, "American children at once responded to the story of the two little

Finns, and suddenly Marguerite knew that writing for children was the writing she had always wanted to do. She has a oneness of feeling with young things, human or other-wise."

Later, in 1940, Marguerite published *Dilly Dally Sally*, a story based on her own childhood. The main character is a little girl who is curious and distractible. Henry and Blackwood worked together again to create *Geraldine Belinda* in 1942. This story is about a stuck-up girl who faces the consequences of her snootiness. In 1943 *Their First Igloo* was released, co-authored by Barbara True, a tale about a brother and sister who get caught in a snowstorm. They work together to build a snow shelter and survive the bitter cold.

At thirty-eight, Marguerite Henry had found her niche. She was just beginning what would become a sixty-year career as a children's book author. But a move to a ranch house with a sizable yard in the small, horse-centric village of Wayne, Illinois, set the stage for her rise to one of the most prominent writers of her day.

At her new country home where neighbors had horses in their backyards, Marguerite began learning and writing about horses. She wanted to know everything about horses that she could, since she had loved them as a child, but never had a chance to be around them. She wanted to identify the different breeds and understand how a giant Percheron work horse differed from a lightning fast Thoroughbred race horse.

And so she began researching for a breed anthology. It was titled *Album of Horses*. As she read piles of books and talked to various horse experts, one breed of horse stood out to her as unique. She went down a research rabbit hole.

The Morgan horse, a short, smart breed named after a Vermont schoolteacher from the 1700s, captivated Marguerite. Although the Morgan was small compared to a large work horse breed, it was super strong. And even though it was compact, it could run like the finest of leggy racehorses.

She immersed herself so deeply in researching the Morgan breed that she decided to write a book focusing on the Morgan. Her first horse book would become *Justin Morgan Had a Horse*. *Album of Horses*, the book she began writing as her first horse book, would have to wait years to be published.

While working on the manuscript for *Justin Morgan Had a Horse*, Marguerite began looking for the perfect artist to bring her characters to life. She searched library shelves for the best horse illustrator she could find. She narrowed it down to two. Will James, author and illustrator of *Smoky, the Cowhorse* had recently passed away. Her other option was an artist named Wesley Dennis. Although the artist lived over seven hundred miles away, Marguerite sent Wesley the manuscript and arranged to meet him in the reading-writing room of a hotel near Central Park in New York.

When Wesley arrived, the first thing he said after meeting Marguerite was, "I'm dying to do the book, and I don't care whether I get paid for it or not." The two had very different working styles, but a mutual love for animals. They became fast friends. Their debut book, *Justin Morgan Had a Horse*, was published in 1945. Over the next twenty years, they created fifteen books together. They became a children's book publishing dream team.

Wesley was a year younger than Marguerite. He enjoyed several horse sports, such as polo, racing and foxhunting. He'd studied horses for years through his job grooming horses for the National Guard. Later, he learned about horse anatomy while studying in France. His charcoal and paint strokes breathed life into Misty, Sea Star, Stormy, Sham and dozens of other of Marguerite's characters. Many of them are unforgettable.

Marguerite and Wesley shared royalties, money from book sales, which is not very common. Together, they visited schools and book fairs to deliver "chalk talks." As Marguerite spoke about their stories, Wesley would draw the characters on a chalkboard or large pieces of paper. Some of those drawings on paper are owned by collectors today.

Chapter 12

The Real Misty Pony

"Just off the shore of Virginia, I heard about a tiny island rising only twenty-one inches above the sea. Wild ponies lived there, ponies whose ancestors had been tossed ashore from a wrecked Spanish galleon. Here, every July when the ponies were done with feudin' and foalin' the fisherfolk of the island staged a roundup ... the biggest wild west show of the east. And so the little island beckoned, and Misty of Chincoteague was born."

Marguerite learned about it after she had published *Justin Morgan Had a Horse* and before she brought Misty home.

The Chincoteague wild pony roundup had been occurring annually for about twenty years when Marguerite's editor, Dr. Mary Alice Jones, attended a dinner party in Evanston, Illinois in the mid 1940s. A man who had just seen it entertained the diners with the drama of the pony swim. Mary Alice listened closely and began peppering him with questions: "Is it a holiday? A pony sale? What is it? And where did the ponies come from in the first place?"

The next day, Mary Alice shared the details with Marguerite and suggested she write her next book about it. In 1946, Marguerite convinced Sidney that she needed a pony for research purposes. She traveled to Chincoteague with a friend who was an excellent horsewoman, Blondie Coffin, to see the island and meet the ponies.

Contrary to the story of *Misty of Chincoteague* in which Misty was born in the wild on Assateague Island, Misty was born in 1946 on Grandpa Beebe's ranch. Marguerite reports seeing the newborn foal lying down beneath her mother. She was instantly in love. "The first time I saw Misty, the tiny filly ... was new as the morning and silky as milkweed floss."

Misty was still a baby at the time, but Grandpa Beebe agreed that once she was old enough, Misty would travel to Illinois to live with Marguerite and serve as her writing inspiration. Eventually, Misty would have to return to the Beebe Ranch so she could have foals. Marguerite paid $150, and the deal was made. The pony arrived in St. Charles, Illinois, via train car on a cold November day in 1946.

When the foal arrived in Wayne, she was covered in dull, fuzzy fur and didn't look like the silky golden horse they'd met in the summer. In fact, Sidney teased Marguerite that Misty looked like a Siberian goat. Marguerite turned her head to hide her tears at the apparent mixup. Nevertheless, she saw that the filly was tired and cold and needed care. Even though she believed Grandpa Beebe had shipped her the wrong pony, she was determined to love her anyway.

They brought the filly to their neighbor's barn, where she was to live until the Henrys could build their own stable. Marguerite spent the night in the horse's stall. "She needed a live, breathing presence in the dark and I'd be there for her." Marguerite brought a blanket and tried to get the filly to eat, but Misty only ate a few bites. Marguerite tried humming to her, but the pony ignored her all night.

As the rainy night gave way to gray morning, Marguerite heard the rustle of straw. Misty approached her! She lay down next to Marguerite. "Her whiskers brushed my palm, then her muzzle was cradled in my hand ... Her animal warmth felt good as she squirmed closer. I was no longer cold. The rain stopped, and we slept." *A Pictorial Life Story of Misty*, published in 1976, retraces how the author and foal met, showing a photograph of Marguerite sitting in deep straw, cradling the just-weaned filly's head as she slept.

When spring arrived and the foal's winter coat shed out, her true colors shone through. She had a white marking shaped like the United States on one side of her body, and on the other side, a splotch "in the shape of a plow, strangely like the state of Virginia." Grandpa Beebe had indeed shipped the right foal.

Before she was trained to accept a rider, Misty learned tricks such as extending a hoof like a horsey handshake and how to step her front two hooves up on a stool and pose. Marguerite wasted no time getting to know her pony and was soon working on what would become her most famous book, *Misty of Chincoteague.*

The book came out in 1947, and it quickly became successful. As more readers got to know the fictional Misty, the real Misty transformed into a celebrity. She made appearances at schools, libraries, book signings and even parties. Marguerite planned elaborate birthday celebrations for Misty.

When the pony was old enough, a local trainer, Eddie Pacuinas, started teaching Misty to be a riding pony. While

Marguerite waited until Misty matured enough to carry a rider, Marguerite met and fell in love with a jet black Morgan horse named Friday. He had been trained to play polo, and when Marguerite took some riding lessons on him, she wanted to bring him home. She told Sidney that Misty was lonely and needed a friend. Now Marguerite had a black horse and a palomino pinto pony in her field.

Misty's second birthday was recorded in a six-page birthday party scrapbook from July 20, 1948. It starts with Misty saying, "Whee! I am 2 years old today. My birthday began with a hearty handshake." The photo shows Marguerite holding Misty's leg right above the hoof (you might recognize it—check out the cover of this book!).

Another caption reads, "Notice the map on my withers. Shows up quite plain here, doesn't it?" The next page says, "I had a party. You should have seen the presents! There were carrots scrubbed clean (even the greens were washed), and a box of sugar lumps, and a bundle of hay and a sheaf of green oats tied with a gold ribbon." A stem of oats is taped to the page along with a small ribbon.

After opening presents wrapped in galloping-horse-themed paper, several of the children rode Misty. Three pictures show little riders aboard the pony bareback. The scrapbook reads, "Everybody was so darn nice about my day that the least I could do was to offer a few free rides. I did a little bucking and kicking so they'd know there was wildness in me. The grownups who watched thought it was maybe a gnat in my ear or horsefly. But it wasn't at all. I'm wild I am! I wanted the children to get a kick out of it."

The last page of the scrapbook is a signed guest list with the names of eleven neighborhood children, some penned in cursive, some in giant scrawling letters of those learning to write. The average age of attendees was 6.5 years old.

***

Mary Jon "Jonnie" Quayle grew up next door to Marguerite and Sidney Henry. When Misty first arrived, she was stabled in the Quayle barn along with their other horses. Jonnie was the first person who ever "rode" Misty. "My sister Nancy and I would hop on her, and ride her bareback without permission. She wasn't famous then … she was just a little horse growing up in our pasture with our other horses." A picture from *A Pictorial Life Story of Misty* shows Jonnie being held over the pony's back. She was about five years old at the time. Even after Misty moved to the Henrys' newly-constructed barn, Jonnie and the neighborhood children were always welcome to visit.

"I loved Marguerite Henry!" Jonnie said in an interview. She remembers walking to Marguerite's house often when she was young. Jonnie wouldn't knock, would just walk right in. "She used to pay me a quarter to make her bed!" Jonnie laughed and wondered aloud if Marguerite unmade the bed in order to give her something to do.

Jonnie recalled Wesley Dennis working at Marguerite's. She saw Wesley sketch Jiggs, the rented burro/donkey Marguerite studied to understand burro behavior to write *Brighty of the Grand Canyon*. Jonnie took home the donkey drawings he didn't like, ones intended for the trash can. Jonnie still has them to this day.

Children loved Marguerite. A 1951 ad promoting the book *Album of Horses* in the *Chicago Daily Tribune* asked the question: "What makes Marguerite Henry's books about horses so popular with children?" Beneath the question is a photograph of a smiling Marguerite riding Misty. The pony's hooves are planted on a small wooden stool.

The ad continues, "Marguerite Henry has what her sister calls her a 'feeling of oneness with young things.' She never writes or talks down to children. Whether she is currying a colt or chatting with a ten-year-old, she treats each with affection and respect. You can get some idea of her popularity with children from the fact that the neighborhood boys bicycle eight miles for the 'privilege' of cleaning her stable. One suspects that the secret of her success in writing about horses comes of having been born an unusually nice human being."

I felt Marguerite's warmth in every photo, article written about her, and in the way her friends spoke of her during my research. I wish I had met this extraordinary person. I had so many questions to ask her about horses and herself. I know we could have been friends.

Chapter 13

Swimming with Horses

Seeing Marguerite with Misty in those old photos reminded me of my horseless childhood and my first experiences riding horses. As a kid, when I wasn't reading one of Marguerite's books, writing horse stories or playing with Breyer model horses, I galloped around my backyard pretending to ride a horse. I jumped over an upside-down picnic table bench with a broom placed in the X of the legs. I cantered from tulip tree to burning bush, then to the far corner of the yard to circle the aspen tree and back to my starting point. I started saving all my money so that one day I could buy a horse of my own.

It took much longer than anticipated to earn enough for my own horse, but thanks to our family friend, Cindy, I learned to ride anyway. One summer when I was almost a teenager, Cindy invited me to help exercise her horses. I would set out on Jim Dandy along with a few other horse-crazy friends and their mounts. I didn't know it at the time, but I was riding very near where Marguerite might have taken Misty out riding.

Our days were filled with riding adventures. There were trails to be explored, jumps to be sailed over and wild black raspberries ready for tasting. With a few dollars in our pockets, we would ride to a small general store, take turns holding each other's horses and go inside to order deli sandwiches and pick up a bottle of pop. We had informal pony picnics within walking distance from Mole Meadow, Marguerite's former home, although by then, my favorite author had moved away to California.

Depending on the season, the purrs of the red-winged blackbird or trumpets of Canada geese followed us as our troupe rode for hours through the glory of the Pratt's Wayne Woods. I'll never forget the time I rode Jim Dandy wearing my swimsuit—not riding breeches and boots. The other girls and I planned to swim with our horses. We trekked along the Prairie Path, a trail converted from a third rail line. We crossed the road and turned down a narrow road.

The homes we trotted by on our way to the swimming hole were the stuff of horse girl fairytales. Several of them had small barns that matched with the grand houses. Riding arenas with colorful jumps dotted several of the properties. I knew this was what heaven must be like (except for the horse flies).

Through a grove of maples and oaks, a small pond shimmered. The water shone like a mirror, but not for long. My riding companions sloshed into the water. Their horses willingly plunged in, and my friends erupted into giggles and shrieks as they became swimming centaurs. I followed, nudging my steed's copper sides with my bare feet.

Jim Dandy good-naturedly joined in the frolicking. When he was in deep enough, the water covered his back. My legs slid out behind me, and I grabbed his chestnut neck in a bear hug to stay aboard. Just as I was getting the hang of this new way of swim-riding, he submerged his head. By the time I realized the possible danger, his head and neck shot up. This friend I had known and loved as a horse transformed into something almost otherworldly, a creature part whale, part marine dinosaur.

I couldn't imagine Jim Dandy had been in a swimming hole before. How did he instinctively paddle his legs once the water was deep enough and have no fear? I remember being terrified when I took swimming lessons at the YWCA when I was four. Where did his seahorse skills come from? If the real Misty had lived on Assateague Island, would she have known instinctively how to swim across to Chincoteague like the Misty in the book?

Chapter 14

Marguerite's Writing Secrets

A 1949 *Publishers Weekly* article described the Village of Wayne where Misty lived with Marguerite for thirteen years and the location of the secret swimming hole as "a strictly horsey, country-estate community. Almost everyone in Wayne has a horse. The children are put in saddles early and, usually, can curry a pony by the time they learn to comb their own curls." From her desk in Wayne, Marguerite penned *Misty* and beloved horse books such as *Born to Trot*, *King of the Wind*, and *Brighty of the Grand Canyon* (which technically is not a horse book—the main character Brighty is a donkey).

Today, Mole Meadow is hidden by towering trees which were likely planted while the Henrys lived there. The three-stall barn Misty lived in still stands. The local historical preservation society receives regular requests from people asking where Mole Meadow is. People still want a glimpse at the field Misty once played in over seventy-five years ago. Out of respect for the current homeowner, the location is never shared.

Marguerite and Sidney loved their small horse farm. She once wrote about her new hometown, "Everyone who yearns to write a book should be fortunate enough to live in Wayne! Source material is just waiting to be mined in every castle and cottage. Experts with the most astounding information are ready to dig up and share the richest nuggets from their past."

As Marguerite became more popular, librarians wanted to know more about her writing methods and inspiration. Roy Porter, who worked for her publishing company, jaunted off to Mole Meadow to interview Marguerite on her writing craft.

On a hot July day, Roy commented how the spacious lawn and beautiful scenery were an inspiring view for a writer. Marguerite replied, "Well, perhaps, but I work with my back to the window so I won't be distracted by horses and hounds."

I was not yet born while Marguerite and her horses lived in Mole Meadow. However, thanks to home videos and even a documentary filmed when she later lived in Southern California, I feel like I've been a guest to her homes.

During my research, I found a movie starring Marguerite Henry. The film shows a slim senior with a pixie hairdo retrieving a stack of fan letters from her mailbox. Marguerite narrated, "When I was a little girl, I wanted more than anything to have a horse of my very own. As I grew older, grownups said I'd get over my longing for a horse, but I never did."

I get you, Marguerite. I never grew out of that horse phase either.

I watched the surprisingly action-packed 1980 film about the writing process. In *Story of a Book*, Marguerite researched in a library, jotted down notes, tapped typewriter keys, drove a Volkswagen van, admired a pinto in a pasture, then spied on her husband. Sidney was reading a first draft of her manuscript on the sunny patio. If she noticed him looking confused or bored, she knew she had more work to do with her writing.

In the film, Marguerite had pep in her step, great posture and wore neck scarves in every scene.

The film taught me that for every book, Marguerite worked through at least five different drafts and enjoyed "revising and polishing a story. It's like grooming a horse to make it shine." After her manuscript had enough "grooming," she would send it off to her publisher. At that point, sadness would fill her. She would only feel better when the manuscript was returned, and she could dive into proofing and correcting typos. She wanted to write with precise words that would create pictures in her readers' minds. I long to do the same.

Chapter 15

Notes Everywhere

What did it take to be a writer like Marguerite? By the end of her career, she had written over fifty books. Three attained the highest honors in children's literature: Newbery Awards. *King of the Wind* won the Newbery Medal and both *Misty of Chincoteague* and *Justin Morgan Had a Horse* won Newbery Honors.

I gained more insight into Marguerite's writing methods when I visited the Marguerite Henry collection at the Children's Literature Collection of the University of Minnesota

Libraries. The archive includes thirty-six boxes of items from Marguerite's life and writing. I could only examine a few boxes at a time, but each one was full of treasures.

Marguerite was always jotting down notes. I found story ideas on old envelopes, scraps of paper, the backs of other documents, and even on a thin piece of cardboard that had been used to keep a tablecloth tidy in its original packaging. It seemed her ideas bubbled up constantly. I learned Marguerite was careful to organize each scrap of paper in folders.

Her sister Gertrude explained it this way: "I think Marguerite has a unique way of working. Instead of making an outline for her stories, she uses a whole riffle of Manila folders, filling them with notes listing what people wore, what they ate, how they lived in the period of her story. The folders are boldly labeled in black crayon and are separated into two groups—those with the plot incidents in their natural progression and those containing background material. One glance at the big black labels gives her a quick visual outline."

For example, in writing *Stormy, Misty's Foal*, Marguerite outlined the story in several folders bearing labels such as "Ponies Huddled," "Misty Evacuated," and "I Feel Blessed; Could have been worse." Marguerite saved a newspaper clipping about the storm that resulted in Misty's living in the Beebe's kitchen as her emergency stall. Underneath, she wrote four lines:

The hard-driven rain slanting under the eaves,
beating on the window pane
At first the rain only plip-plopped
cold bitter rain. Practically snow.

The scene for Stormy's birth was drafted with penciled phrases on the back of the draft pages from *The Wildest Horse Race in the World*, her 1960 book. A yellowed newspaper clipping was secured onto an old page along with several notes. Her writing evolved as mixed media art.

Wesley Dennis once wrote, "This ability of Marguerite's to inspire a new reverence for seemingly simple, everyday things is a particular gift of hers for which I am grateful. An old halter, a candle snuffer become more fun to draft after Marguerite has described them."

Marguerite found inspiration from many sources. She particularly enjoyed reading and continued copying down memorable quotes, just as she had as a child.

Chapter 16

The Struggle to Write Well

I'll never forget sitting on the back porch as my middle sister Renee read about how the little boy in *The Carrot Seed* walked off with the world's largest carrot. His mom, dad and brother had told him the carrot seed he planted wouldn't grow, but the boy kept watering it and pulling weeds day after day. Renee read the book to me so many times that one day,

I recognized the words and could follow along as she told the story. I could read!

I started writing later, and I've now published several books. Writing is usually harder than reading, as Marguerite knew well. She confessed in unpublished notes for the anthology *Something About the Author*, written when she was eighty-six years young, "My writing life wasn't always easy. There were apprentice years when I wrote sixteen geography books, each one took at least six weeks and was paid $25 per book. My cleaning lady at that time earned the same amount once a week working from 8 to 1, although I'll have to admit my work was more fun."

A fan named Brian wrote to her asking, "Is it hard to be an author, or is it fun? I would like to know this because I am writing my first book." Marguerite replied, in Newsletter #4, "Dear Brian, It is both. Some days when your characters behave and everything goes right, you wouldn't change places with anyone in the world. But there are days when you tear up most of what you write. Even then, you know you couldn't be happy doing anything else."

Marguerite had many setbacks. She recalled an assignment early in her career that seemed to take forever to write. After "interruptions, interruptions, interruptions," she finally submitted it, only to learn that her publisher no longer wanted it, because a competing magazine had just published a similar article. Nevertheless, she persevered, just like the little boy in *The Carrot Seed*. She decided to get help. "In white fury I sat down at my typewriter and banged out letters to big name writers who were not scooped … How, I asked them, do you find peace and quiet? How do you escape the little gnat-like interruptions that pick away at time and thought? What are your work methods? In short, how do you bridle Pegasus?" She mailed twenty letters asking for advice to Eleanor Roosevelt, George Bernard Shaw, Thornton Wilder and Somerset Maugham, to name a few. All of them wrote Marguerite back.

Much of the advice she received is still helpful today. I battle with writing and ignoring distractions every day. Instagram notifications and an email stream pique my curiosity when I attempt to have a single focus of stringing words together. A desire to make a Nespresso, text my friend, watch a funny video, or check out the latest group message pull me away from my paragraphs.

It's nice knowing I'm not alone; Marguerite struggled with distraction too.

Irish playwright George Bernard Shaw told her, "I began my literary career without the means to choose my surroundings. I had either to write under all circumstances or not to write at all."

Shaw, who penned *Pygmalion*, the inspiration for the beloved musical *My Fair Lady*, and later *Saint Joan*, a play that garnered him the 1925 Nobel Prize for Literature explained, "A very considerable part of my plays were written while on railway carriages between King's Cross and Hatfield; and it is no worse than what I have written in the Suez and Panama Canal."

Marguerite didn't write from the Suez or Panama canals, but once from a fire hydrant, another time from a department store glove counter, and even from a ladies bathroom and fitting room. One day, upon discovering that she didn't have her notebook for a very important interview with a high ranking partner of a pocket watch company, she listened to the man carefully. Immediately after the interview she grabbed paper towels from a ladies bathroom, and wrote a flurry of notes onto them. Unfortunately, this story didn't last: "A week later when I returned home, I confidently took the sheaf of towels out of my bag. What consternation upon preparing to write the story to find that all of the writing had disappeared!" She had to rely on her memory to complete the news story.

From Thornton Wilder's letter, Marguerite learned another trick of the trade. The author of *Our Town*, and a three-time Pulitzer Prize-winner, said, "When you are held up in plot or character development, get out and take a walk. Stride and tramp out your material." He also shared a Gertrude Stein quote: "It takes lots of loafing to write a book."

Marguerite didn't quite follow his advice, but she thought of a similar strategy: "I climb aboard my black horse Friday and trot and gallop it out. Occasionally, we meet up with screaming fire trucks or huge mechanized corn pickers. Then Friday bolts and flees while I hang on for dear life, prayerfully, breathlessly singing, 'Jesus loves me, this I know ....'"

After those breathtaking rides, her mind would become clear. "The hurdle which blocked my progress miraculously, almost mysteriously, disappears."

It's amazing how many problems can be solved from horseback.

Howard Vincent O'Brien, a journalist, replied to Marguerite, saying, "This peace and quiet business is mostly nonsense. It is an evasion practiced not by people who write, but by people who would love to have written." It seemed to him that people who asked for silence were usually using noise as an excuse not to write, and most such people would never become real writers.

Marguerite disliked peace and quiet. She claimed she was unable to write alone. After all, she'd learned to write in the middle of a busy kitchen. She liked the feeling of others around her also working.

Her writing companions didn't have to be human. Her Dachshund Alex often worked alongside her. "His self-appointed task is with the wastebasket." The dog would remove pages from the basket one at a time and tear them "into infinitesimal bits, so that I can never be tempted to retrieve a discarded phrase." If Sidney ran errands with the dog, Marguerite would "dash off to a library" so she didn't have to work alone.

The years Misty lived with her, Marguerite wrote from 8 in the morning until 1 p.m., then went outside to be with her horses. Marguerite hand-wrote all of her books, stating she felt happier with a pencil in her hand, as "it is almost like caressing the words." She would hire a typist to take her cursive manuscript to typeface. When Marguerite released a new book, Sidney would have one copy bound with a leather cover, making it a one-of-a-kind edition.

I wish I knew the whereabouts of Marguerite's special collection of leather-bound books.

Another writing challenge Marguerite grappled with was golf. Sidney loved golf and often brought her along on long golf holidays. Marguerite wrote to a friend about one memorable holiday. Another couple had come on the golfing trip. The wife was an avid golfer who insisted Marguerite play every day. "I felt as frustrated as a horse on the wrong side of the fence because 18 holes on a very difficult course laced with water hazards and gouged with sand traps is sheer torture for me. I took two or three strokes to everybody's one."

There was an Arabian horse ranch an hour from where they were golfing with a mare who had just given birth to healthy twin foals (which is a rare event). "Every time I dubbed my shot, I yearned to do a story about those twins, but I never even saw them!"

Still, she didn't give up.

Just as she persisted in golf, she was persistent in her work. *Misty's Twilight* was originally written in first person. The publisher asked Marguerite to change the point of view to third person. She rewrote it. She was ninety.

Marguerite, who yearned to be an expert at her craft since girlhood, had learned to bridle Pegasus. We readers, writers and horse lovers are able to enjoy the results of her hard work.

Chapter 17

Research and Cozy Details

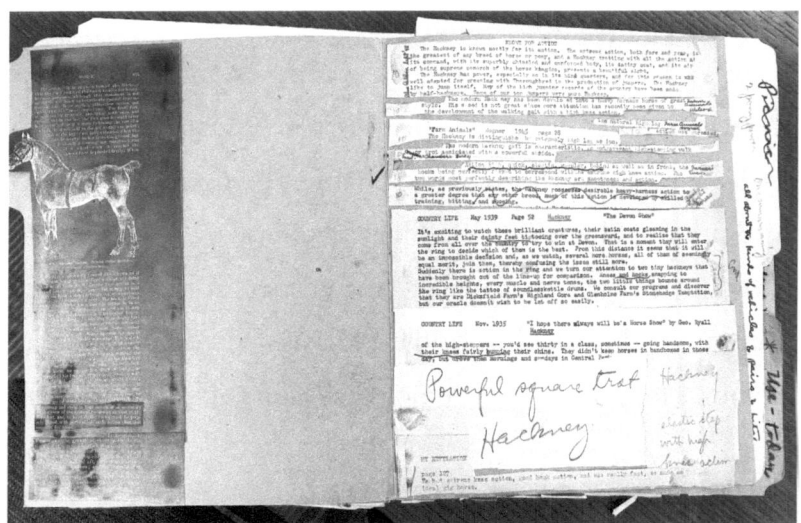

A 1949 *Publisher's Weekly* article read, "Marguerite Henry spends months and months on research work for each of her books. She writes thousands of letters gathering the necessary material. Every detail must be accurate, every statement true, each word the right one with the perfect connotation." This is amazing to me because Marguerite relied on letter writing, people and paper to craft her stories based on fact. She did not have the internet. There were no search engines or personal computers. Marguerite would talk to people in real life or on the telephone. She would go to libraries and read, read, read. Plus she would often travel to the location where her story was based.

One of her research folders for her book *San Domingo: Medicine Hat Stallion* shows her dedication to accuracy as well. The folder was stuffed with all these items:

- Two square Kodak snapshots of Independence Rock

- 2 stenographers paper's pages worth of notes about Independence Rock

- 18 pages photocopied from a book *Independence Rock: Great Record of the Desert* with images showing names carved into the rock

- 1 page of typed notes taped to the back of a battery company advertisement

- 1 bookmark-sized paper with a sentence about Independence Rock

- 7 copied pages from the aforementioned *Independence Rock* book taped to the back of price lists for Cornell paperboard products with red underlines and annotations in the margins

- 2 pages of typed, summarized notes about the rock; one observation in black cursive states, "Independence Rock is a low horizontal rock shaped like a French loaf of bread."

- 1 page of photos of Ezra Meeker, the man credited with saving the Oregon Trail

- 1 large copied image of Independence Rock

- 1 poem "Independence Rock' by Addie E. Holmbery of Lader, Wyoming

- 2 pages of notebook paper with a red title of "weather" and "buttes? or mesas"

- 1 description "A big boulder looks like turtle at water's edge," on a scrap of paper

- 1 more page of handwritten notes

- 1 more page of typed description of Independence Rock

- 4 more scraps, bookmark size and smaller, of rock description

- 1 postcard of Independence Rock

Marguerite invested hours of research in Independence Rock even though it's only mentioned five times in *San Domingo: Medicine Hat Stallion*.

Details helped Marguerite's stories come to life, and she was diligent about fact checking. In one letter from 1976, Marguerite wrote to a man from the Chincoteague Volunteer Fire Company asking for help remembering details about the *Misty* movie premiere in 1961, fifteen years earlier. Marguerite was in the middle of writing the book *A Pictorial Life Story of Misty*.

Her letter began, "Readers love cozy details so they can picture a scene as if they were right there." Like a teacher assigning homework, Marguerite included six pages, each with two or three questions at the top of the page followed by blank spaces for a response. One page starts like this: "I remember Miss Victoria Pruitt helping to raise money to buy uniforms for the High School Band. I'd appreciate knowing the colors of the uniforms in 1961. Would the band have played some special numbers?"

It's understandable that she might forget the uniform's color after fifteen years, but she also noted she'd had other things to focus on. "I remember the parade vividly—BUT FROM ONE ANGLE ONLY." Misty was in the lead, walking with Uncle Ralph Beebe. They were followed by a stallion named Silver King, hitched to a pony cart.

"Wesley Dennis and I were in the cart, Wes driving. Silver King may have been gentle to ride, but I don't think he'd ever been driven before. He took off at a gallop for Misty. His check strap broke, and he tried to kick the cart to kingdom come. Fortunately, a roundup man on the sidelines had a piece of thong [leather] in his pocket. He stopped the pony, Wesley repaired the check strap, and we took off again, both of us feeling that at any moment the strap would break again. The spectators were laughing hilariously, and Wes and I were laughing hysterically. Now you know why I don't remember much about the parade. I was too busy hanging on!"

Chapter 18

Traveling to the Setting

While researching her book *San Domingo: Medicine Hat Stallion*, Marguerite journeyed over much of the Pony Express route herself, writing to her editor Mary Alice Jones that she took several hundred pictures of "landmarks, way-stations, etc. My desk is heaped high with literally pounds of material. The sifting and sorting is, of course, still going on and will for weeks to come. I like to spend my daytimes on this material, including the books, pamphlets, and articles culled from museums, bookstores and libraries along the way. All of these preliminaries I am enjoying to the full, letting the pieces fall into place before beginning the actual writing."

Once a story idea grabbed her, Marguerite traveled to the setting and recreated the experiences her historical characters faced. Inspired by an article about a heroic burro, Marguerite took Sidney to visit the Grand Canyon one Valentine's Day morning. It was only five degrees, and Marguerite was nervous about the narrow trail they would ride to the bottom of the Grand Canyon. Then the guide gave her a mailbag. She reasoned that the mail always got through, so she was able to enjoy "the splendors of the ride." Meanwhile, Sidney was unusually quiet. Marguerite thought he was simply too amazed to speak, but actually, he was terrified of heights. This freezing cold ride became a part of the book *Brighty of the Grand Canyon* in 1953.

Marguerite was curious to experience what her characters would feel. She once "sampled the burro browse that grew up in sprigs up through rock crevices; I had to know how it would taste," and hiked part of the trail so she could picture how Brighty would have made the climb. She also camped in the same cave where President Roosevelt, Brighty, and Uncle

Jimmy Owen spent the night. The sound of a mountain lion awoke her. "Terrified, I dived deep into my sleeping bag, like a headless turtle." The next morning, Marguerite spotted the lion's large paw prints. That near-cat experience helped her build a scene full of suspense and danger in her book.

Another story idea inspired Marguerite to travel across the ocean to Italy. For her 1960 book *Gaudenzia, Pride of the Palio* (later published as *The Wildest Horse Race in the World*), Marguerite had to see the "mystic, mad, wonderful race of the Palio": two summer horse races held in Siena, Italy, in the city center. During the race, jockeys ride without saddles and horses dash around the sharp corners of the town's medieval-era public square.

Marguerite began researching, and after saving up for two years, she flew to Italy and spent time with the locals to learn about the history and culture of the Palio. Marguerite did not speak Italian, but she could make herself understood with hand gestures. In *Dear Marguerite Henry*, she confesses to persuading a young banker to be her translator. "With my interpreter, I talked to the Captain of the Guards, the chief magistrates of the contradas, the official starter of the race, the Palio veterinarian, newspaper editors, professors, and even to His Holiness, Pope John XXIII. Each one gave me a piece of the story until everything fitted neatly into place." While her translator was busy at the bank, Marguerite struck out on her own. I can picture her seated at a feast table surrounded by Siena locals high with the excitement for the upcoming horse race.

When I opened a box in the Marguerite Henry Collection and found a collection of souvenirs from her trip to Italy, I could almost imagine Marguerite's joy as she brought the treasures home and examined them. I pulled out a sky blue and white jockey's cap. Nestled with it was a photograph of Giorgio the jockey, wearing the same cap, seated near his parents. I held up an oxhide whip used in the race and found Italian calendars with images of Palio races. I even saw a *spennacchiera*, a horse's headpiece that was shaped like a plump horse show ribbon. In the center of the rosette, a broken mirror still shone.

A note on the inventory list read, "This is the actual spennacchiera worn in the Palio by Gaudenzia when she won, alone, without a rider, for the contrada Giraffa." I was delighted to find a letter from a teacher who wrote to thank Marguerite for lending her these artifacts for a class project.

Marguerite loved collecting things, but they weren't just mementos. Each item helped to make her story more real. Once home, Marguerite prepared for the writing. "I get out a big bulletin board and then I fill it and the desk with all the photographs and other mementoes I've gathered connected with the story and its locale. This helps me to steep myself in the atmosphere of Siena and the Palio or whatever I am writing about—it is like telling the story from my experiences as though I had lived it myself."

Chapter 19

Library Adventures

Although Marguerite loved to travel and do research on-site, her constant companion was her local library. "My happiest working hours are spent in the library ... there is the miracle of seeing the thin, tangled thread of information which I bring in with me become untangled and laid out in a straight line ... the library is a kind of holy place for me."

While she was feverishly taking notes, librarians passed by and helped people, which reminded her of friendly teachers. "They believe in me. They charge the whole atmosphere with encouragement and faith."

Like Marguerite, I spent many hours in the library. My adventures there began long before my serious research days. In second and third grade, my best friend Gail and I would go to our local library and hang out for hours. This was in between playing with our Breyer model horses and cuddling her cats. I was not allowed to have a pet in the house, which made horses the best choice: it's definitely a pet you don't keep in your house. Unless you are Marguerite Henry. She trained Misty to enter the house and allowed her to eat grain off the seat of a chair. The mare was welcome inside to meet guests and even enjoy a Thanksgiving and Christmas with her human family.

I first met Sea Star in the children's section of the library in Elgin, Illinois, as well as Brighty, the burro. In the book room for grownups, Gail and I explored the Dewey Decimal areas of 636 (animal husbandry/horse care) and 798 (equestrian sports). We had to learn how to groom, tack and sit in a saddle, so we'd be ready for the blessed day we'd become horse owners.

Without the library, horses might not have charged into my life, forever changing who I am and how I see the world.

Although doing all that research might have sometimes seemed like a daunting task, Marguerite always found little things to keep her excited. In a newsletter, Marguerite considers the question of whether her research was hard work: "Would you call it work to have handwritten diaries brought to a private desk of your very own? Diaries written over a hundred years ago? Some are in brownish ink, some in pencil, yet all in such nice and precise script that they are amazingly easy to read. Quite suddenly, you are transported into the past."

In order to learn as much as she could, in the Huntington Library in Southern California, Marguerite read fifty handwritten diaries dated from 1834 to 1875. They had been written by men and women traveling mainly from Pennsylvania, Wisconsin or Illinois to Oregon territory. "It was the intimate details of the people's experiences—their hopes, fears, dangers, tragedies, joys that made them thrilling and important. I felt as if I were an emigrant too, walking alongside the wagon trains, helping to bury the dead, assisting at births, fording or ferrying across streams ... In order to walk in another's boots and in another era it's good to know what his heart and mind are feeling too. That's what I found in those long ago diaries."

Marguerite was a hands-on learner. Her curiosity about bluebirds drove her to raise mealworms in laundry tubs in her basement. By observing the "blue forget-me-nots of the air" in her own backyard, she authentically described their habits in her book *Birds at Home,* published in 1942.

This was not the only reference book she composed after extensive research. Marguerite began collecting information about horse breeds for a guide that would eventually become her book *Album of Horses.* Her enthusiasm for horses and their histories led her to "exciting studies in libraries—borrowing books, ten at a clip and poking around in the stacks for more." After months of library research, reading and jotting down notes, she took her research on the road.

"With a bundle of notebooks and a camera, I charged across land and sea—from the Arabian Ranch in Pomona, California, to the Morgan Horse Farm in Vermont: from Thoroughbred and Standardbred stables in Kentucky to the Lipizzaners in Austria." She enjoyed speaking with all manner of horse people, from famous riding instructors and horse owners to farriers, cowboys and even circus trainers.

Marguerite's love of libraries, learning and adventurous spirit trickled down to her readers. I should know.

Chapter 20

Fan Letters and School Pictures

Although Marguerite received many awards for her writing, the praise she loved best came from the letters she received from young readers. Forty file folders in the Marguerite Henry archives are full of fan letters. More than anything else, these letters show what kind of a person Marguerite was.

Alice Crowson sent a letter to Marguerite in 1979. "What I like is that you don't make the story boring by writing 'horse ran over the river, through the valley, across the plain (yawn).' Your books are exciting, full of life and fun and parts that make you laugh and some that make you cry, beautiful, wonderful parts that fill you with a precise picture of the scene and they always leave you feeling warm and like you know the person (or horse)." Crowson's enthusiasm for Marguerite's tales could not be contained into a sentence governed by standard English conventions. Instead, it burst into a heartfelt run-on sentence.

I feel the same way, Alice!

Another letter from an eighteen-year old big sister says, "Remember me? I've written to you before." (A number of letters contained the "remember me," indicating Marguerite had repeated correspondence with some fans.) She described how her little sister had received a copy of *Misty* for Christmas and asked if they could read it together. The teen shared with Marguerite, "I was so enthusiastic about it I couldn't stop reading and they wouldn't let me. My stepmother and even my father sat down to listen until I had finished the book. I read the whole book in one day and enjoyed every minute of it."

What a cozy family scene! It struck me as unusual that a sixth grader wanted her older sister to share the story. The teen had seen Misty in person, so perhaps the younger girl knew she would be able to make the story come alive.

Most of the letters I perused had the abbreviation "ans." in cursive in an upper margin. I am pretty sure it was Marguerite's way of noting which letters she had already answered. Replying to fan mail was of supreme importance to Marguerite—so much so that while she was traveling, her sister Gertrude would reply to fan mail on her behalf. Marguerite was quoted in a newspaper article as saying she believed each letter from a child was a sacred trust. Children responded to her warmth by sending her all kinds of questions and often asking for advice.

One boy wrote to Marguerite and explained that his father had gotten rid of his best friend, his horse, without telling him. Marguerite wanted to help the boy in the only way she believed she could. We learn in her short film, *The Story of a Book,* she decided she would write a book just for him and make the main character a brave boy, a Pony Express rider. Marguerite elevated her hurting fan to hero status as Peter Lundy in *San Domingo: Medicine Hat Stallion*.

In the late 1960s, Marguerite launched a newsletter as a way to connect with fans and reply to their most commonly asked questions. The debut newsletter began, "Dear Readers and Riders: Well it finally happened! So many letters I didn't know what to do. I felt exactly like the old woman in the shoe.

Here were children's letters full of questions so exciting that each one required a special answer." At the bottom of the page is a photograph showing Marguerite reading a letter. A mound of fan mail covers her desk. Next, the newsletter had two articles: "Brighty Becomes a Movie Star," and "The Story Behind the Lipizzan Story." It ended with responses to six fan letters covering questions such as how long it took her to write a book, and whether or not the book *Sea Star* was true (it is "based almost wholly on fact").

My favorite letter read, "Dear Miss Henry, I have a question to ask you if you don't mind. Do you think it is right to kiss a horse on the nose which you love dearly?"

The author's response was, "If he doesn't object, why not?"

Fan mail continued to roll in. In the ninth edition of the newsletter, Marguerite announced that she was planning on writing a question and answer book. In 1969, Rand McNally released *Dear Readers and Riders*, with a subsequent edition titled *Dear Marguerite Henry*. Newsletter #9 explained her new book was dedicated "to every one of you who have ever written a letter to me. Even if your specific question is not included, you have contributed to the book because you took the time to sit down and write out your thoughts and feelings about reading and writing, and horses and riding, and foxes and burros, all manner of things."

Finding the newsletters was like uncovering buried treasure. A librarian near Mole Meadow handed me a blue folder containing nine photocopied newsletters. I was shocked when he said I could check out the folder as if it were a book. I saved them on my phone so I could review them as many times as I liked.

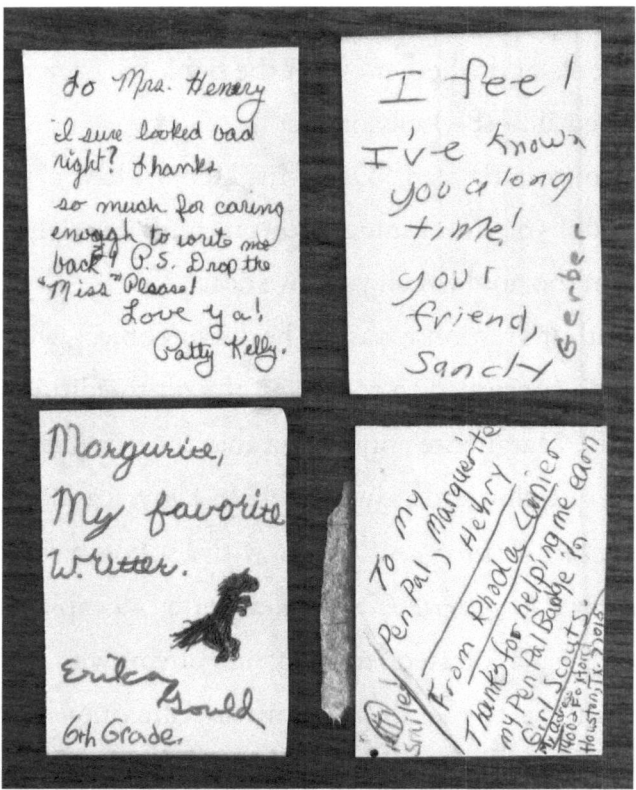

With the letters, children often sent Marguerite pictures. I opened one file folder to find a sea of wallet-sized school pictures: a mosaic of horse lovers spanning decades. There were a few black and white photos of girls wearing cat eye glasses and some in John Lennon-style wire rims. Many of the snapshots were yellow-hued early color photos from the 1960s. The 1970s were represented by long, butterfly collars and feathered hair.

The pictures spread out before me represented just one folder: number two of ten. Marguerite had saved around 1,800 school photos from children.

I turned many of the photos over to read what was written on the back. One little girl's school picture said,

"To Mrs. Henry,

I sure look bad, right?

Thanks so much for caring enough to write me back.

P.S. Drop the 'Miss' please!

Love ya! Patty Kelly"

A school photograph from a fan from Houston read, "To My Pen Pal Marguerite Henry, From Rhoda Lanier. Thanks for helping me earn my Pen Pal Badge in Girl Scouts."

Another school picture said, "I feel I've known you a long time! Your friend Sandy." Marguerite seems to have added Sandy's last name, making sure she'd know how to address the envelope when she wrote back.

The photos weren't always formal school pictures. I found many snapshots of children with horses, frequently named Misty or Stormy. One showed a young cowgirl with orange bows riding on a thick palomino. She beams from under her straw hat. She captioned it: "Patches and I at horse show (we didn't place)." In pencil, Marguerite wrote the name of the girl, Vickie Vandervoort, along with, "You placed in my heart." The word "heart" is underlined.

On occasion, entire classes would write to Marguerite. A 1979 letter from a teacher said, "When you saw this postmark, I'm certain you thought, 'This is a familiar town!' Obviously, my students read and enjoyed Misty, which prompted the 'flood' of letters you received recently. As their teacher, I wanted to write and say thank you for your replies. The children realize how lucky they are to have received personal replies from you, and have eagerly shared those replies with all of us. Few people care to take the time these days, particularly when children are concerned. But we truly appreciate your thoughtfulness and we say thank you, from all of us."

Lauren Hoeffner wrote to ask if she had a favorite book of the ones she had written. Marguerite, ninety-two at the time replied, "I don't have a favorite book. I'm like a mother with many children. I love each book-child for a different and very special reason."

Bonnie Shields, who illustrated Marguerite's last book *Brown Sunshine of Sawdust Valley*, told me how important the fan mail was to Marguerite. "You would be amazed, even at her age in her nineties, she got letters and letters and letters from little children. And they would all put a little drawing in it and she had them posted up in her office. She was always changing them because she was getting them forever. But they were always there and she always got a lot of delight out of them. She was the real thing, honey. She was the real thing."

Marguerite not only loved each book-child, but also the children who wrote her or befriended her in real life. Her last newsletter reminded children to read *Dear Readers and Riders*: "Wherever you read the book—in your home or at your library—I hope you will know at once that it was written for you; it is my way of saying, I love you."

Chapter 21

Young Friends

When Ed Richardson was around ten and Marguerite fiftyish, she paid Ed seventy-five cents an hour to ride and care for Misty. It was his first job. Another neighborhood boy named Tex Drexler would ride Jiggs on trail too. As the trio strolled along the country lanes, Marguerite would try out storylines on her riding companions. If Ed and Tex liked her ideas, she would use them. She had her own tiny, trotting focus group.

"So, what was Misty like?" I was dying to know, but I'd saved the question until the midpoint of our meeting to try to seem more sophisticated than the fangirl I am.

"She was a mean pony."

My heart sank.

Misty was the stuff of little girl pony dreams! How could I break her fans' hearts with this news?

Ed confessed he got dumped by Misty frequently, and she would try to bite when he'd tighten the girth. And Misty wasn't the only naughty one: Jiggs would often sit down like a dog, and Tex would slide off to the ground. Marguerite was the only one who ever rode Friday.

"Why do you think Marguerite picked you? I would think all the local kids would want to ride the famous pony."

Ed replied that Marguerite had noticed him playing with her dog and recognized him as an animal lover. She was correct, and even though Ed never became a veterinarian like he'd planned, he continued to love animals all his life.

As we chatted, we looked over a photocopied letter from Marguerite to Ed. Little Bub, Misty, Sham, Sea Star, Rosalind and Brighty—the main characters from several of her most popular books gazed back at me from the letterhead. The letter, dated July 14, 1991, was written when Marguerite was eighty-nine. She explains, "I'm sure you will understand when I tell you the reason for my slow letter-writing is because

I'm busy book-writing. Somehow I can't seem to do both at once! Misty's Twilight is my current project, and it's taking shape nicely."

Marguerite shared that the riding adventures with him and Tex "pop into my mind frequently, reminding me of those magical years in Wayne. Writing about Misty's Twilight, a spunky descendant of our Misty, brings those warm memories into sharp focus and tickles my face into a Grandpa Beebe grin, wide and happy." She also told him to hug his newborn son for her and to sing Onward Christian Soldiers to him, a hymn the Wayne trio of riders would sing together on trail. She closed the letter with, "in my heart you will always be my dear trainer, friend, riding pal and co-singer Eddie. And that's how it shall remain."

"You were very special to her," I said.

"She always treated me like I was an adult, but I was only ten. She was really special."

Ed opened a small box. A pair of bronze button-looking items, about the width of a golf ball, lay next to a small pine-themed Christmas card. It read:

These were worn by Tony Welling's famous Skippy (see p. 26 of the Album of Horses). Merry Christmas, Marguerite Henry

The bronze buttons had once gone on the bridle of a bay police horse in Cleveland, Ohio. *Album of Horses* tells the story of what could have been a tragedy when a circus caught fire. A brave policeman and horse rode into the flames and led a herd of circus horses to safety.

Ed explained how much Marguerite loved doing pony publicity, and he mentioned how much he liked Sidney, even though Marguerite's husband wasn't around much.

Over the course of the next year, Ed and I exchanged emails. Whenever I had a question like, "How tall was Marguerite?" (he said she was around five-foot-seven) and "Did you ever meet her sister Gertrude who answered mail for her?" (he didn't), Ed responded rapidly.

We met again, almost a year to the day of our introduction. This time around, he had a scrapbook to show me. It started with an invitation to a party. A small note in the corner read, "Dear Eddie—Don't forget the day. M"

Misty of Chincoteague and Brighty of the Grand Canyon are coming to the Children's Christmas Party. They will put on three playlets with an all-star cast:

Uncle Jimmy Owen played by William Winquist [a local horseman]

Maureen Beebe played by Eddie Richardson

Paul Beebe played by Tex Drexler

Misty, the pony, played by herself

Bright Angel, the burro, played by himself.

For each child there will be a Christmas gift in Brighty's pack.

It seems especially appropriate to have Brighty, the burro, with us at this season, for was it not a little long-eared beast that Jesus chose to ride into Jerusalem? Legend says Jesus wanted to reward his patient burden bearer, so he marked him with the emblem of the cross. And ever since, the burro has worn a dark stripe down his back and withers over his shoulders for all the world like the symbol of the cross.

If your children would like to trace their fingers along Brighty's cross and gaze into his wistful eyes, he will stand very still, returning the adoration in full measure.

A large Santa Claus with a text bubble announcing, "I'll be here too!" seemed to be an afterthought. What a party that must have been.

"Did neighbors think Marguerite was eccentric, bringing Misty into the house and having parties with a pony?"

"No. Everyone loved her, " Ed told me.

I asked him if Misty was naughty during parties. He replied, no—the little pony would do anything for Marguerite.

***

Eddie and Tex weren't the only local kids who spent time with Marguerite and her animals. I'd already met Jonnie Quayle, Marguerite's neighbor. Another of Misty's young friends was Richard Beltz. He met Marguerite in 1949. His teacher introduced him to the book *King of the Wind*, mentioning the woman who wrote the story was a local author. Richard and a buddy found their way to Mole Meadow, and they began to visit three to four times a week.

Richard, alongside his friend Denny, pedaled his red Monarch eight miles one way on a mostly flat country road to see Misty. It took him about an hour each direction. He would help Marguerite by cleaning her yard or brushing Misty and Friday. Marguerite would make her young friends and helpers sandwiches.

All the neighborhood kids were welcome in Marguerite's home, and she treasured their friendship.

Chapter 22

Influence Before Influencers Existed

Marguerite was both serious and warm. She took it upon herself to teach children that they were special and loved. She said it constantly through her books, letters and in person.

Ann Keckonen recalls meeting Marguerite, who was a distant relative. "She was a lovely friendly lady, and she considered all the children who visited her and Misty to be her children." Marguerite's warmth made her very special to her fans. If she were alive today and active on social media, my guess is she would have hundreds of thousands, perhaps millions, of eager followers.

Marguerite and Misty were dedicated to spending time with their fans. They visited schools, libraries and even Marshall Fields department store on State Street in Chicago in order to sign books, stage skits and meet fans.

It's not clear if Misty's many appearances were Marguerite's idea or her publisher's, but the Chincoteague Pony wasn't the only animal who visited fans with the goal of helping to sell books.

An elephant named Judy dressed up as Eddie the Elegant Elephant in 1944 to help sell copies of *The Elegant Elephant*. She held a hand stamp in her trunk and "signed" copies of the picture book. Apparently, Judy was reluctant to leave the store and ate the Indian corn on store displays before exiting.

Another animal, Zip the chimpanzee, made appearances in 1953 to help sell *Zippy the Chimp*. He wore shoes, pants and a shirt with "ZIP" written across it. The little ape roller skated and rode a bicycle on the *Ed Sullivan Show*. Misty's appearances began after Eddie/Judy the elephant and ran concurrently with Zippy. It seemed that Rand McNally was invested in live animal guests to help market its books around that time.

Although Misty never appeared on *Ed Sullivan*, she went on the road to promote the film Misty, inspired by her life. In Hollywood starlet fashion, she left her hoof imprints on the sidewalk in front of the Chincoteague Island movie theater in Virginia. You can see them in the concrete today.

Everywhere they went, Marguerite and Misty found dedicated fans. Marguerite welcomed them all. In a 1951 WLS Chicago radio interview promoting *Album of Horses*, Marguerite said, "Misty has a birthday party every July 20th. I never send any invitations but everybody is invited … Children can see her and she shakes hands, and then always she has to have a little handout of oats." On air, she invited Wesley Dennis to come to the birthday party. He said no "That's the middle of summer. I'm always trying to catch a fish at that time."

"Well, you might catch a birthday cake with carrot tops for candles," Marguerite teased.

Local newspapers would run articles about the pony's upcoming birthday, and fans sent a "shower of greeting cards" addressed simply to Misty at Mole Meadow. Marguerite hung up the pony birthday cards on the wall of Misty's stable, declaring, "she seemed to enjoy looking them over."

Publisher's Weekly reported on Misty's seventh birthday party. "The first ... was attended by 20 people. This year there were almost 400 guests, and they brought Misty tributes which included a set of gold-plated horse shoe nails, 84 bunches of carrots and quantities of sugar lumps, apples and cookies."

Each child received a piece of chocolate cake baked in a horse shoe mold, and Misty received a birthday cake made of oats, sugar, molasses, chopped walnuts, and carrots turned upside down as candles. The recipe for Misty's Oat Cake is found on page 50 of *A Pictorial Life Story of Misty*. I made the cake for my horse Knight's seventeenth birthday, and served it up to him on a fancy platter. He ate the carrots with gusto but did not want to try the cake. My sister and I shared the cake—it was delicious.

In a short film taken at one of the birthday parties, you can see an ocean of children seated on a hillside looking down at Misty. She performs tricks, and two neighborhood boys take the parts of Maureen and Paul Beebe to act out a short scene from the book *Misty*. Next, Marguerite's burro, Jiggs, appears with a man, and the two act out a scene from *Brighty of the Grand Canyon*. Jiggs is wearing ketchup on his legs because in the story, he's just survived a mountain lion attack. Apparently, "He couldn't help licking the catsup, which always brought down the house." The film ends with Marguerite giving Misty the carrot-candled cake.

As much as she delighted in pony parties and Misty meetups, Marguerite was not just about having fun. Beyond celebrations and special events, Marguerite used her influence to both educate children and encourage them to become involved in their communities. After the success of her 1966 book *Mustang, Wild Spirit of the West*, Marguerite told young readers about wild horses and the dangers they faced. *Mustang* told the life story of Velma Johnston, also known as Wild Horse Annie, a Nevada secretary who fought for protection of America's wild horses.

In Marguerite's Spring 1967 newsletter, she shared that men were caught chasing wild horses by plane. This was not only terrifying for the horses, but it broke the law. She urged children, "You can help. Everybody can. Write to the Bureau of Land Management in Washington, D. C., reminding its members that there is a Federal Bill that forbids the horrible roundup of wild horses by plane, and that you, the boys and girls of our nation, ask that the law-enforcers uphold it." And write they did.

A year later, the fall 1968 newsletter began, "Dear determined letter writers, I am glad, proud, and grateful to all of you for the new explosion of letters you sent to the Bureau of Land Management about the wild horses up in the Pryor

Mountains ... the way you peppered the Bureau with our protests and pleas has brought a big victory."

The newsletter then showed a copy of a letter from the Bureau. They had set aside a huge area of land as a wild horse sanctuary. It's still there to this day.

Around this same time, Marguerite and Bob Lougheed, the illustrator for *Mustang, Wild Spirit of the West*, bought two Spanish Mustang fillies and donated them to a living museum in Oklahoma City. They wanted children to see in real life, the horses that shaped our nation, the protagonists of *Mustang*.

In her next newsletter, Marguerite asks for help getting a Mustang refuge near the Colorado-Utah border. Today, pintos and palominos, blue and red roans, bays, grays, sorrels, blacks and a few Appaloosas frolic in the Little Book Cliffs

Wild Horse Area, a 36,000-acre range just outside Grand Junction, Colorado.

Marguerite's fans had changed the world again.

Chapter 23

Chincoteague Pony Fun Facts

Through Marguerite, horse-lovers all around the world learned about the plight of wild Mustangs out West and the charm of the wild Chincoteague Ponies in Virginia. To this day, folks visit Chincoteague to discover the truth about the ponies made famous by Marguerite Henry and Misty, and remember the author's warmth and stories. Some start by visiting the island and never leave.

"It all started with Marguerite. A lot of people have Misty in the back of their minds when they figure out the pony swim is still going on. It's not overly commercialized, and Chincoteague still has a small town feel. The way they do the auction is still the same. Cowboys bring foals out and you raise your hand to bid," said Allison Dotzel. I interviewed the veterinarian and Chincoteague Pony owner as I was preparing to visit Chincoteague myself.

At the time of our conversation, there were nineteen stallions on the island, but not all of them had bands, as some of them were still too young. Clusters of young stallions are kicked out of the band they were born into when they are old enough. They hang out together with other young stallions in bachelor bands until they are able to woo mares of their own and begin their own bands. Thirty ponies lived in the southern area of Assateague, and the rest of them stuck to the more remote northern area. In order to see ponies of the northern territory, visitors have to hike several miles up a long service road.

Allison is an expert on the Chincoteague Ponies. She told me that the wild ponies are not only rounded up before the famous pony auction, but they're also gathered on Assateague every spring and fall for veterinary care. Pony fans come to see this too, but it's much less crowded than Pony Penning Week in July. I knew the Chincoteague Volunteer

Fire Company owned the island herd, but I discovered they're more involved than I would have guessed.

For example, it's a little-known fact that not all ponies make the summer swim: mares too pregnant, foals too young, or horses too old are herded into trailers and driven to the Chincoteague carnival grounds. But not all foals have to be trailered. Foals only a few days old can sometimes be seen sloshing in the water near their mothers. They grow up playing in the surf. The fire department keeps careful watch over the herd. If a pony has health problems, they bring it from Assateague to Chincoteague for special care.

Every year, a committee composed of Chincoteague Volunteer Fire Company members meets to decide which foals will be auctioned off and which foals will be auctioned but returned to the island. Foals that are purchased for naming rights and then returned to the island are called "buybacks." Usually the committee chooses fillies as buybacks, and they try to choose ponies that bring something unique to the herd. The committee also decides when a foal will be old enough to leave its mother. Every colt or filly born by July is sold, but the younger ones will be allowed more time to grow up alongside their mamas.

People can support the ponies in a lot of ways. They can donate money, and sometimes groups of friends get together and pool money to purchase a buyback pony and gain naming rights. Allison explained, "People are excited about their part in the history of the pony." Although they don't keep the pony, buyback purchasers are photographed with the foals and receive official registration papers.

The ponies that do go home with buyers aren't just mementos of *Misty of Chincoteague*. Allison said, "I've seen them cut cows, event and drive, or be used for 4-H, trail ponies and companion ponies. They do just about everything."

After talking with Allison, I couldn't wait to see the ponies myself firsthand and experience the wonder of the event Marguerite called the "Wild West show of the East."

***

Before my trip, I discovered there's a Chincoteague Pony Names app. You can see all the ponies on the island in the app and browse their photos, videos and history. You can also search for ponies by their gender, color, brand, face, leg and pinto markings. If you're on the island, this makes it easy to identify the ponies you're seeing. Horses related to Misty have a special notation in the app. Money from the app is donated to the Chincoteague Pony Rescue.

I love being able to follow my Chincoteague Pony crushes conveniently from my phone.

The Chincoteague Volunteer Fire Company relies on donations and sales to pay for care for the ponies. Just as Marguerite and Misty played a role in putting Chincoteague on the map in the late 1940s, this app and other social media platforms help horse lovers discover and admire the ponies. And fan support really helps. In 2021, a buyback pony was sold for $25,000, which isn't unusual. The highest-selling foal at the time of this writing was a 2023 brown and white pinto filly that the buyback "owners" named SCC Misty's Hailstorm. She sold for $43,000.

Marguerite realized early on that Misty's legacy would live on. "The dynasty of Misty will continue as long as there are children who remember the golden pony with the map of the U.S. on her withers." Not only children but adults remain dedicated Misty fans. Misty's foals and their descendants continue to live free on Assateague Island. It doesn't seem likely that fans will forget them anytime soon. Each glimpse of ponies playing in the sea or lazing on the sand, and every rowdy foal, whether seen in real life or via photos and videos inspires delight.

Chapter 24

Pony Penning Prelude

As I drove on the causeway leading to Chincoteague Island, I tilted my sunglasses down, sure they were falsely filtering the view. Nope, the yellow-green grass was just that vibrant. White egrets on stilt legs strode along areas of low tide murk. Dozens of billboards for local businesses greeted me. The word Chincoteague comes from a Native American phrase for "beautiful land across the water," a perfect description.

For many Misty fans, going to Chincoteague is a life goal. I hadn't given it much serious thought. When I read the books as a child, it didn't occur to me that I could actually visit Misty's home. But then I started researching Misty's story for this book.

In *Dear Marguerite Henry*, the author described Chincoteague Island's annual Pony Penning.

"All year long wild pinto ponies roam free on Assateague Island. Then along comes Pony Penning Day, and a bunch of men who were fisherfolk yesterday turn cowboy today. Loading their own horses on a scow, they cross over from Chincoteague to Assateague and put on the biggest Wild West show in the East! Through marsh and bog and briar they ride hard and fast, spooking the wild ones out of hiding, driving them to Toms Cove. It's like a tidal wave seeping all the ponies to one spot where they can blow and catch their breath … the water churns with ponies—stallions bugling to their mares, mare neighing to the colts." Once the ponies have crossed the water, they're herded right down Main Street to the carnival grounds.

Pony Penning Week is a big deal on Chincoteague. Thousands of spectators from near and far gather to see the wild ponies. I needed to see it for myself. Admittedly, I could have gone to one of the smaller roundups in spring and fall when the ponies get health checkups. I could have avoided the traffic, but the timing worked out better in July, so I began searching for a hotel. I also booked a kayak rental for the day of the Pony Swim and a boat ride for the Friday swim back to freedom.

Three days before the Pony Swim, I turned right onto Main Street, driving slowly to take it all in. On the right, a tall painted sign for Chincotiki Bar and Grill caught my attention for its cute wordplay. On the left, a red brick building stood: the historic Chincoteague Fire Department. Just beyond it was the tiny Island Theater. Its old-fashioned marquee advertised daily showings of the *Misty* movie and a Thursday night screening of *National Velvet*, a classic horse movie. I clearly had a lot to fit in this week.

Before I reached my hotel, I spotted a bronze statue of Misty. She was shown as a playful foal version, tail flicked up and frolicking with a duck. I didn't see any more evidence of ponies, but I knew I was so close.

I had met my first Chincoteague Pony the day before near Middleburg, Virginia en route to the island: a coal black mare with white hooves named Cricket. She was a 2001 Pony Penning "alum." Her handler, Katrina, told me about the pictures of Cricket as a foal swimming the channel and trotting down the street to the carnival grounds. Katrina recalled her trip to Chincoteague seeing the ponies several years earlier, reporting that all the foals she saw were "smart, brave, athletic and straight-legged."

My eyes widened when Katrina said, "I read *San Domingo: Medicine Hat Stallion* to my son when he was little, and after that, he wanted a horse like that." He was hoping for a pinto, a horse with large spots, one of the spots appearing on the top of his head coloring both ears—a medicine hat. Katrina said, "I found our medicine hat gelding Odie for sale on Facebook."

A book Marguerite had written over fifty years earlier had influenced this family's horse shopping! I was certain this wouldn't be the last time I'd see Marguerite's influence around Chincoteague.

Chapter 25

Face to Face with Wild Ponies

The next morning, I drove to Chincoteague National Wildlife Refuge on Assateague Island. Cars were pulled over so their passengers could gaze at the ponies. The southern herd of about thirty mares, stallions and adorable foals milled about in a corral. I spied the ridiculously good-looking stallion Riptide drinking from a water trough, but I don't think he saw me, as his eyes were both covered by his thick forelock. I used my app to identify Little Miss

Sunshine, a palomino pinto mare with a lightning-shaped star, and her tiny lookalike filly.

A sign outside the double fence said "Do not ever feed the ponies! You can kill them! Horses and ponies have weird digestive systems that are not like people, cats or dogs. They can COLIC or FOUNDER which causes great PAIN and even DEATH if they eat things that don't agree with their tummies. Too much green grass, grains (like corn, sweet feed), "treats" like apples, carrots or human food can be deadly … Chincoteague ponies have centuries of evolving and adapting to a salt marsh/barrier island environment and giving them anything out of their ordinary diet can make them very sick … If you see a sign we mean it! If you see a pony don't feed it! Thank you, CVFD." I'd make sure to keep my snacks to myself!

The wild ponies seemed anything but. Even the foals, who I guessed had never been this close to humans before, calmly nursed, napped or tasted grass and hay. Cars, people, and even photographers didn't seem to bother them. They were beautiful.

After I had taken several photos of the herd, I drove to Tom's Cove, the setting for a key scene in *Sea Star: Orphan of Chincoteague*. At the visitor center, I was just in time for a birdwatching talk. "Summers are for pony people, and spring and fall are for bird people because you can see their migration," said the park ranger.

She mentioned that the ponies' bellies look a little bloated. This is because of the cordgrass they eat. I also learned that Assateague Island is part of both Maryland and Virginia, and the states manage their respective herds differently. The Virginia part of Assateague Island is surrounded by fencing for the ponies' safety. The Maryland part is completely open. This means that the ponies sometimes go to beaches in Maryland and bother beachgoers. I had seen YouTube videos of people disregarding the warnings about the wild ponies by getting to close to them and trying to pet them, and getting kicked. "That's what you get for disobeying the rules," I thought and tried not to smirk.

Chapter 26

A Walk on the Beach

On the Monday of Pony Penning Week, my alarm went off at 3:30 a.m. I had to get up early to head down to the beach. A benefit of getting up so early was I would get to watch the sunrise before the northern herd ponies began their beach walk down to the corrals on Assateague. At the corrals, the wild Chincoteague Ponies would join the southern herd for the big swim on Wednesday. Park rangers were already at the parking lot directing other horse-crazy tourists.

As I rummaged in my car for my beach chair and towel, I noticed a woman in the car next to me doing the same thing. She made the drive from Atlanta by herself just for this special event.

We walked in the morning darkness, talked and found spots in the sand behind a rope meant to section people off from wild ponies. My new friend had never heard of Marguerite Henry and Misty, but she had heard there were wild ponies on an island you could glimpse with your own eyes. She gushed, "Last year I spent forty days skiing. I think I would like to ride a horse one day. I love going fast!"

The sunrise was magnificent. The sky morphed from black to smoky gray to pale blue as the sun forged its path into the sky. As we waited for the ponies, I learned more about the event. A woman in a red windbreaker told me that everyone working at the Chincoteague carnival would be Saltwater Cowboys. She explained that nobody gets paid; it's as though the volunteer firefighters do their day jobs in order to support their passion of being volunteer firefighters. Most families on the island have at least one family member who is a volunteer firefighter. When you hear the fire alarm go off and see firefighters rush out, frequently it's not a fire, but a pony in distress. They diligently care for the ponies. They deliver hay to the wild ponies if it's a harsh winter. If water holes dry up in summer, the firefighters' powerful fire horses will top off the watering holes.

The windbreaker-wearing woman said some pony buyers end up with "a very expensive lawn ornament," but other ponies become best friends. She told me about a teen she knew who had worked the last two years to raise money to buy a Chincoteague foal at the auction that week. She abandoned the idea of buying a car to afford her very own pony. I remembered my days as a horse-crazy teen working small jobs to save up for an equine best friend.

I also met a woman who introduced herself as a Misty fanatic, Breyer horse collector and model horse show judge. When I told her I was writing a book about Misty and Marguerite, she pulled out her phone and showed me a picture of her Misty Breyer model on the steps of the Beebe house. It was the same house where Misty spent a few days living in the kitchen during the deadly storm in 1961.

At 6:54, the waiting crowd stood, and soon we could see three Saltwater Cowboys loping on a palomino, dapple gray and bay. As they shot past us, cheers rose above the waves and wind. Next, two four-wheelers followed and around a dozen more Saltwater Cowboys. Behind them, a giant cluster of riderless ponies walked and trotted along. The Chincoteague ponies knew the routine.

Shouts of "Hey! Hey! Hey!" and "Yah!" and occasional shrill whinnies burst above the sound of the waves. More Saltwater Cowboys rode the beach side of the herd, guiding the ponies at the water's edge. I looked for the foals, but they were hard to see. They stuck close to the sides of their mothers.

A brown and white pinto broke away to trot ankle-deep into the ocean. A cowboy turned his horse back to cut him off. The pony pivoted and splashed back toward the end of the line. The pinto, who I learned later was Norman Rockwell Giddings, was not trying to escape the roundup. As a young stallion, he was likely trying to stay away from the drama of older stallions and bossy mares who might bully him.

I quickly snapped a selfie with the stream of ponies behind me. Within minutes, the herd passed. Along with hundreds of other spectators, I turned to watch until I couldn't see them anymore. The march of the herd happened so fast, but it was worth it. The experience filled me with joy.

Chapter 27

Chincoteague Pony Superfans

After the pony beach walk, I met Rebekah Hart and Amanda Geci, founders of the International Chincoteague Pony Association and Registry. Rebekah lives on a family farm with her herd of eight Chincoteague Ponies, one of them a Misty-descendent stallion. Amanda is a walking encyclopedia of all things Chincoteague Pony and can name all the ponies and cite family trees.

"I've been coming to Pony Penning for twenty-seven years. During the winter, I go on YouTube and find random videos from old news reports or educational films where there is a clip about Chincoteague Ponies, and I will ID them from that."

We spoke as we watched the northern herd and southern herd mill about inside their respective corrals. Two stallions groomed each other, muzzle to withers. I couldn't believe how gentle they were around the foals.

"Usually stallions are pretty cool until they're given a reason not to be," Amanda explained.

We started discussing stallions, and she told me Don Leonard and Hoppy's foals tend to be a bit taller. We also chuckled about horse behavior: "There's one cantankerous old stallion who swims his band out to Pope's Island. It's nearby and small, so they don't have to compete for grazing. He knows how to take care of his women."

We discussed horse training, and I learned there was a Chincoteague Pony Drill Team. It was hosting an open house the next day, and I knew I had to attend.

I learned the Chincoteague Pony Association was making plans to give out awards for owners to get the ponies properly trained. Raising a pony isn't always easy, but many folks wanted to see the ponies receive the care and education they needed to live dignified lives away from the island. Goodbye expensive lawn ornaments.

Marguerite would be proud.

The next morning, I walked to a park to meet up with a Chincoteague walking tour group. Two women with graying hair asked me to take their picture as they posed next to the bronze Misty statue. They cheerfully told me they weren't horse people, but they'd come for Pony Penning Week because of Misty. Their second grade teacher had read *Misty of Chincoteague* to the class.

I was amazed. Decades later, Marguerite's story still affects readers, even those who didn't love horses. My connection to Chincoteague was a little more obvious, but thanks to the *Misty* book and the beautiful story of the ponies, hundreds of people had heard about this special event.

The tour guide began, "If you're not familiar with *Misty of Chincoteague*, it's a dream of a story."

I couldn't have said it better myself.

Chapter 28

Games on Horseback

Five flashy pintos and a palomino with a white mohawk mane trotted around KerKaKen Acres riding arena during the Chincoteague Pony Drill Team open house. The teens rode bareback to blaring music. When the song suddenly stopped, riders leaped off their ponies' left sides, bolted around them and swung up on the right.

The palomino's rider, unable to remount before the others did, was out. She led her horse to the middle of the arena, where he placed his front hooves on a platform, striking Misty's signature pose. The music started up, and the game continued, a horseback version of musical chairs, until a winner was declared.

Next during the open house, a fundraising free-for-all occurred. Spectators along the arena held out cash—donations for the drill team. Riders rode around trying to collect as many dollar bills as possible. I held up a couple of dollars, and a teenage rider snatched them from my hand and galloped off to drop the bills into a bucket. The excitement was contagious, so I reached into my purse and pulled out more singles.

Finally there was a cakewalk, which was like a version of musical chairs, but instead of walking around chairs, you were supposed to walk around the riding arena. Rebekah urged me to join them. The cakewalk entry fee was a dollar, and the prize was a Misty's Twilight Breyer model horse signed by Maureen Beebe. As a little girl, Maureen was written into *Misty of Chincoteague* as a main character. I meandered around the arena as music played, feeling like I belonged there. I had arrived on the island alone just a few days earlier not knowing a soul. Everyone I'd met had welcomed me as a fellow pony-lover. I didn't win the cakewalk model horse prize, but I felt a part of something positive, even if I was only a small part. My attendance at the open house and my small cash contributions were being used to keep the story of Misty going for current young readers.

Although I've been a horse girl for most of my life, there have been times I've felt like an outsider. When I was a teen, the local riding instructor told me I couldn't join Pony Club because I didn't own the horse I rode. I was devastated. As an adult in California, I was ready to start taking riding lessons again, but despite many emails and phone calls, only one horse trainer replied. Even though I was an experienced rider, I was left out of horse communities. I'm now well beyond the age of being chosen for teams on the playground, but the Chincoteague Pony crowd made this middle-aged Thoroughbred owner feel like I already belonged to their community.

Some time after the cakewalk, Amanda walked with me to the announcer's booth to meet Kendy Allen, who had founded the Chincoteague Pony Drill Team and owned the farm hosting this event. She also owns Misty III, also known as M3. I got a picture with the taffy and pearl mare as though she were a celebrity. Amanda introduced me to Kendy, and I told her about the book I was writing about Marguerite Henry. Kendy was happy to share.

"Marguerite Henry was my friend. When my daughter was little, Marguerite would call from California—it was late here—around 11 o'clock. I would wake my daughter up to talk to her. I would hear giggles from the other room while they talked. It warmed my heart."

I wondered if Marguerite had forgotten about the time difference between coasts—she would have been in her late eighties—or if time wasn't important when she was feeling creative.

Kendy had been to Chincoteague Island several times during her thirty-eight years as a 4-H leader, traveling with groups of children. They would observe the wild herd as proof ponies don't need to be pampered. She would go on to write several books about Chincoteague Ponies.

In 1988, Kendy learned that Misty II was for sale. The thirteen-year-old chestnut pinto mare was Misty's granddaughter. Tourists would visit the pony farm where she lived, reach over the stall door to pluck strands from her mane. She had earned a reputation as a rogue and had never even been trained to ride.

"She was the most beautiful pony I had ever seen, and my husband encouraged me to buy her."

Misty II traveled to the Allens' farm. "She was one of the best ponies I've ever had in my life." Misty II became a show pony champion, and all of Kendy's children eventually rode her. Kendy decided to write a letter to Marguerite.

"My letter said you might like to know we still love Misty, and we have one of her offspring, and she is a super pony. One day—it was the time of day with four kids around, everything would unravel—I was getting supper ready before my husband came home from work. The phone rang, and this very sweet voice asked, 'Can I speak to Kendy Allen?'" It was Marguerite. "This is somebody, and here we were in a rinky-dink, rainy-roof farm in Lancaster County Pennsylvania, but she called back, and our friendship just grew."

Although they never met in person, Kendy and Marguerite formed a lasting friendship. They wrote letters and talked on the phone. The two bonded over their love for ponies, books and children. Today, Kendy owns the largest herd of Chincoteague ponies in the world, save for the Chincoteague Volunteer Fire Company. She is passionate about ponies and loves showing how the formerly naughty Misty II was intelligent and eager to please once she'd had a little training.

Kendy and family eventually moved to Virginia because of the ponies. She managed the Chincoteague Pony Centre for years. Today she is both preserving the Misty line and providing opportunities for young people to meet, love and ride the ponies. She founded the Chincoteague Pony Drill Team and helps organize events for young riders, including holiday parades and fun shows. Misty's Thunderstorm, Misty's Sunfire, Misty's Irish Mist and Misty's Heart of the Storm—all descendants of the real Misty of Chincoteague—make great ambassadors for their breed.

Chapter 29

The Pony Swim

On the day of the Chincoteague Pony swim, I prepared with extra mosquito repellent and sunscreen, even though it was cloudy. I'd tried hiking on Assateague Island, but I had to turn back after fifty yards since mosquitoes were attacking my ankles and flying around my head. Their shrill warnings buzzed in my ears. I was prepared to enjoy myself during the pony swim, at least, and set out in my rented kayak. Jing, the woman I'd met on the beach at the sunrise beach walk, paddled next to me as we passed boats that had been waiting in the channel all night. We cruised past private docks, single and double-story homes and an "island" of black mussel shells clumped together. A pontoon driver passed us with a wave. In the distance, the red and white striped Assateague lighthouse reached into the sky high above the woods.

After about twenty minutes of paddling, we arrived at a wide expanse of water. We wove between pontoon boats to get to the floating boundary line where we tied our kayaks. I had a front row seat to the pony swim lane! The tide would go out over the next two hours, leaving the water slack (with no current). This was the safest time for the ponies to swim across.

Under normal circumstances, a two-hour wait for anything would seem unbearable, but the history and charm of the setting, plus the energy of my fellow spectators gave it a sense of magic.

I had read an account of the time Marguerite Henry and Wesley Dennis attended the pony swim while researching to bring to life the *Misty* book. This was in 1946, and the two had made plans to take their cameras to different places along the swim so they could get photos from two different perspectives. When the swim was over, they met up. Neither of them had taken a single photo. Both author and illustrator were too fascinated with the unfolding drama. Fortunately, we got *Misty of Chincoteague* anyway. I knew I needed to document this event, so my iPhone camera was at the ready, but I didn't want to spend my time staring at a phone screen. I focused the camera on the water and then left it so I could witness the ponies sloshing through the salty water with my own eyes.

A crowd had gathered along with me. A mother and daughter had traveled from Boston with a camera. Near a green canoe, a dad stood on a sandbar playing with two little kids wearing arm floaties. An Amish or Mennonite family dressed in dark garb sat together in a silver fishing boat.

Another nearby kayaker told me Marguerite Henry is the reason she owns horses today. When she's not driving her horses, she travels with a group of friends on riding vacations around the world. I asked her if she would be picking up a pony at the auction.

"No, my husband watched me leave to make sure I didn't go down the driveway with my truck and trailer."

Shouts of "Hey! Hey! Hey!" rang out interrupted our conversation. The Saltwater Cowboys, in the lead on horseback, with the famous, beloved Chincoteague Ponies were headed our way.

My kayak swayed while the ponies streamed past. They seemed to be only about a car's length or two away from me! Foals set their heads on their mothers' rumps to rest mid-way through the swim. The rhythmic purrs of their exhales filled the air as they glided right past me.

The swim itself was quick, like a horse race, like the beach walk from two days earlier, but the excitement lingered. Stallions and mares and foals reached the muddy bank of Chincoteague. They rested for about an hour before the Saltwater Cowboys guided them down the street to the carnival grounds. That, too, was like a parade. I didn't get to see it, but I would not have traded my front row kayak seat for anything.

Meeting other pony enthusiasts made the experience all the better. As I began paddling back, I met a young woman who, like me, had road-tripped from the Midwest. She'd heard about the event from a friend and was enchanted, so she asked off work and camped in her truck. She had never read *Misty of Chincoteague*, nor was she familiar with Marguerite Henry's books, but the very idea of the swimming ponies called to her, beckoning her to their marshy home.

Chapter 30

Bidding on a Foal

On Thursday of Pony Penning week, it was time for the foal auction. The auctioneer spelled out the ground rules for the sale. "Foals numbered forty-three to fifty-seven will not be available to go home until August 27, and fifty-nine on up not until October 1." The littlest foals would still have time to spend with their mothers before going home with human families. He continued, "We will accept cash, MasterCard or Visa. You have no excuse not to buy a pony."

A Chincoteague Pony Drill Team rider on a chestnut pinto pony led the team around the foal pen to an instrumental version of "The Star Spangled Banner." Next, the auctioneer instructed, "Everybody raise your hand. When you want to bid, leave it there." The crowd was filled with excitement. Even though I wasn't there to buy a pony, the event was thrilling.

To my surprise, the foals weren't the only things being auctioned to raise funds for the Chincoteague Volunteer Fire Company. A tiny crocheted baby firefighter outfit was on the block, and later Maureen Beebe's English saddle, a fifty to sixty-year-old Stubben, sold for $7,400. When the last item sold, foal number 1, a coffee-brown pinto filly with a blaze, appeared. Three volunteer firefighters kept close to her, making sure she didn't run scared through the ring. The winning bid belonged to an online bidder for $2,750. The auctioneer cried, "Sold!" and the crowd erupted with applause.

When bidding started for a palomino pinto filly, a little girl with braids and festive face paint raised her hand. After some back and forth with other bidders, the auctioneer boomed, "Sold!" The little girl and a gray-haired woman sitting next to her smiled at each other and walked toward the auction booth to pay for the pony. The child's pink T-shirt read, "Nana said I could."

A pinto filly with blue eyes and a wide blaze appeared in the ring. The top of her mane was milky white while the bottom stuck up in a milky chocolate color. A piece of rope around her neck listed her as number 12. The auctioneer was quick to announce that she was a Misty descendant, just as he had for some of the others. An online bidder won the pony with a bid of $9,000.

It was impossible to pick a favorite foal. They were all so cute. Some had red spray paint on their side, some green, and some had no paint. The red meant they were buybacks, and the green too young to be separated from their mothers yet. No paint meant they were good to go.

During the auction, I became friends with another pony fan. She wore purple sunglasses and told me she had three "very sweet" Chincoteague Ponies who were part of her ten-horse herd. She was there bidding on a horse for her mother, who had first introduced her to Chincoteague but couldn't come to the event. I have never vacationed anywhere with people so eager to talk to strangers and form friendships. It was very different from my experience being denied Pony Club membership as a girl.

After the auction, I received a message from the woman with the cool sunglasses: "My mom won number 12. Misty descendant."

I wondered why an elderly woman in a wheelchair wanted a young wild pony. But I pondered it, and I think I figured it out: this pretty pony was both a link to a powerful story and a dream. Misty's blood runs through the blue-eyed filly's veins. In this great-great-great-great grand-foal of a pony heroine, delight, joy and love live on. Perhaps the aging woman was holding onto that joy, no riding required.

In the introduction to *The Illustrated Marguerite Henry*, Charles Hillinger, a journalist, talks about Marguerite. "I first met Marguerite Henry in Chincoteague, Virginia, and she was not even there. I was covering Pony Penning Days on World Wide Events for the *Los Angeles Times*. Families had driven for miles not only to watch the wild ponies swim from Assateague Island to Chincoteague, but also to buy a young colt to take home. Many of the children were clutching a book and told me about their friend, Misty of Chincoteague, with such enthusiasm that I determined to meet the author in person."

I feel like I met Marguerite on Chincoteague too. This wasn't my first meeting. I'd gotten to know her through her books and my research. But I met her in the smiles and stories of the people who loved her, and in the colorful ponies.

Chapter 31

The Swim Home

Long before my visit to Chincoteague, I visited a stable near San Diego where a friend kept her horse. I didn't know it at the time, but chatting with some folks at the stable would lead me to location of the house in California where Marguerite Henry had moved when she was in her late sixties. I had driven past the street without even realizing it, and I'd even been in the area signing books a while back.

I got to chatting with a young woman a few stalls over who recommended I talk to her friend Sara. "She works on one of the boats that takes people around the island to see the wild ponies. Tell her I said hi." Sara had fallen in love with Chincoteague Ponies and the island itself a few years ago and had moved from California to the island. She began working for a boating company that takes tourists out on the water to see the ponies. She'd met and married a Saltwater Cowboy.

It was incredible to think that someone could be so inspired by Marguerite's books that she'd first brought a pony from Virginia home to California, then moved across the country to start a new life and spend time with the Chincoteague Ponies. Sara wasn't the only one who loved Marguerite and Misty.

***

The morning of the swim back, the Friday of Pony Penning Week, dawned clear. The crowds had somewhat dispersed, but there were still scores of boats near pony swim lane. A pod of dolphins played in nearby waters, their shiny backs gliding in and out of the water. Perhaps they too were celebrating the ponies' return home.

"Are you Sara?" I asked a smiling, very pregnant woman on the boat anchored next to mine. She confirmed she was and invited me to hop onto her boat. We had been texting, and I was eager to meet her in person.

Just like when I'd met other Chincoteague Pony lovers, it felt like we weren't strangers as we shared our horse stories. During our conversation, I found out the pony she'd bought while still living in California hadn't been her first pony purchase. The story was so sweet I could imagine it appearing in one of Marguerite's books.

She explained that when island life on Assateague becomes too difficult for the wild ponies, they are retired to a farm on Chincoteague. One old mare, blind in one eye, had been brought to the farm with an injured leg. She was in such bad shape she was scheduled to be euthanized. When her caretakers came to give her her last meal, they found a foal by her side. No one had known she was pregnant. The colt was a complete surprise! Motherhood worked wonders for the mare, and she healed enough to eventually rejoin the island herd. Her foal had given her something to live for.

In a way, the Chincoteague Ponies do the same thing for people who love them: they give us a sense of purpose and hope. Even though I don't have a Chincoteague Pony myself, reading about them and exploring the history of the most famous of all Chincoteague ponies and her Number One Fan, Marguerite, gave me a sense of purpose. The ponies had also helped me connect with others like me, and I felt welcomed and understood by those who still adore Marguerite.

Sara bought the senior mare's miracle colt directly from the fire company, and over the next few years the mare delivered three more healthy foals. She died of natural causes in the wild on Assateague in 2021.

After chatting with Sara, I stepped back to my boat and sat with my feet in the water. I chatted with fellow horse-lovers as I waited for the ponies to return.

"Oh wow! Look at them," a man behind me shouted. A colorful cluster of mounted Saltwater Cowboys and a now smaller Chincoteague herd walked and trotted onto a grassy area at the water's edge. This time, the wild ponies, not the Saltwater Cowboys, led the way.

"There they go!" the man burst out. The swim back happened so fast, I'm glad I captured it on video. Six ponies plunged into the shallows. Behind them, nose to tail, more ponies followed. Without any hesitation, they surged forward chest-deep, then neck-deep into the channel. With ears perked and muzzles above the blue, the equine pumped their legs, each underwater stride drawing them closer to Assateague. The cowboys didn't have to guide them. The ponies knew where they were going: home.

A sea of blazes, stars, stripes, snips and some solid-colored faces with no white at all chugged forward. A few boats sailed alongside them, far enough away to give the ponies space but close enough to watch out for them.

"Look at that leader, it's cutting through the water!" a man pointed out to a toddler. Once the ponies had passed, our tour boat started moving to keep in sight of them. We stopped when the ponies reached Assateague's shore. One pony flopped down and rolled, hooves to the sky, body wriggling from side to side. Kayakers were able to paddle close, getting front row seats to the gleeful homecoming.

Now cantering and splashing along the marsh's edge, the ponies passed the kayakers. Two gulls swooped overhead as one pony paused to graze. Another small troupe doubled back farther on land, organizing into their bands.

"They're so happy!" I proclaimed. And it was true. The ponies were home together, wild and free on Assateague. I was happy too—happy to be there and drink in their celebration along the water's edge, where they will continue to gallop and play and swim, delighting generations to come. I was so grateful to Marguerite. Without her books, I might never have known about this glorious homecoming.

Chapter 32

A Website for a Pony

As I was looking for other Misty fans, I couldn't help but be impressed by MistysHeaven.com, a site that "strives for updated and accurate information on the Misty family line, as well as offering many photographs of the ponies themselves ... information to make the Misty fan happy!" For over twenty years, Matt DesJardins has been running the website.

Matt has loved horses ever since he was young. As a kid, he couldn't have a live horse of his own, but he loved Breyer models and horse books. Marguerite's were his all-time favorites. He'd chosen a copy of *Misty of Chincoteague* as his prize for a third-grade reading contest. "Misty on the cover is very inviting; she's almost smiling at you. I chose it, read it and loved it. It was a two-part thing for me, leading me to reading more of Marguerite's works. I looked in the back of the book and went back to the library for *Sea Star* and *King of the Wind*."

Matt explained, "The thing that really ignited the Misty interest was I was in the library in the non-fiction section. I saw the book *A Pictorial Life of Misty*, and I thought, 'I wonder if that's the same Misty.' I learned Misty was a real pony. It wasn't just a story. That Misty book was the origin of the website and its descendants. They're all real and they have similar weather names. Then I got the Breyer models. Misty's a pivotal part of my life."

Matt received the Misty II Breyer model horse set for his sixteenth birthday, and he wanted to know if this Misty was real too. He began exchanging letters and emails with Kendy Allen, who owned Black Mist, Twister and Misty II—all three ponies in his set. After a while, Matt began working on the Misty website. He was still a teenager, but he spent a few summers at the Pony Center in Chincoteague and even rode in the drill team open houses. They were some of the best summers of his life.

Because of Kendy's kindness and encouragement, Matt had the thrill of riding two of the ponies from his Breyer set, Black Mist and Twister. However, his favorite pony, not part of the model horse trio, was Misty's Heat Wave, Misty II's eighth known foal.

"She was a beautiful palomino, and we just clicked. Misty ponies are so whimsical, as I discovered with Heat Wave. She was reliable, she was mellow and she was just an amazing pony. Her Misty lineage was the icing on the cake. Did I like her because of Misty? Yes, but I liked her more because she was wonderful." All these years later, Matt still has a picture of his favorite Misty descendant hanging on his wall.

During his Chincoteague summers, when he wasn't working with Kendy's ponies, Matt set off for Assateague Island to search for wild ponies. "There I was staying at Kendy's with a paddock full of ponies, but I would go over to the island." He couldn't help loving the wild ponies then, and his fascination with them continues to this day. "Even though time marches on, the island and the ponies are always still there. They're still doing the roundup. Misty's descendants are still among us today."

Matt's interest in Misty's family tree drove him to learn computer coding even though he does not consider himself very techie. "I had a friend who created a model horse website. I told her I was interested in starting up a website for Misty's family ... my friend taught me how to do html codes."

As the site was being built, Matt met Amanda Geci online. This is the same Amanda who co-founded the International Chincoteague Pony Association and Registry. They bonded over their pony interest. Matt asked Amanda to write for and to help maintain the Misty's Heaven website.

Matt was the one who selected the name Misty's Heaven for his Chincoteague Pony family tree website. "I was in my late teens, trying to think of a culminating name to bring it all together. We basically made the website for us, Amanda and I joke. I go back to the website to scroll. It's like your whole family is in heaven, all the horses being together in one place. Plus, if you're a diehard Misty fan, it is like heaven. I thought it was a neater way rather than saying Misty's Website."

I asked Matt why so many people still love Misty after all these years. Matt is pretty sure it's because the story is so real and unique. "Seeing them swim across the channel is amazing. I remember thinking, 'Wow this is it!' I remember my first swim. It's the experience, and part of that experience affects certain people. Why did I spend several years tracking down Misty descendants? I don't know. It was just so neat—a family tree. These ponies were related to this famous pony. It's the legacy, and there's a certain kind of magic to it."

Misty of the Chincoteague isn't a completely true story. Misty wasn't born on Assateague, a wild pony; she was foaled at the Beebe Ranch, and the Phantom, Misty's dam, was never set free. But Chincoteague is real. Like the rhythm of the waves lapping Assateague's shore, the pony swim happens every July, as does the foal auction.

Marguerite created a storyline that resonates today. She recognized that many people, especially children, long for a horse of their very own. A horse or pony will never judge us or tell our secrets. Some people collect paintings or sculptures or grow flowers. An equine partner is dazzling, textured art on four hooves. Their breath is sweet, their nickers kind. Our horse and pony friends demonstrate for us how to live in the moment. By riding them, we borrow their strength and swiftness. Our saddles are a gateway to something like freedom. Peace, purpose, community, beauty.

No matter how much time marches on, no matter how much readers change, no matter how much tragedy we face, the Misty story, the ponies and their peaceful island remain the same. The wavy-maned creatures nibbling on marsh grass, striding by the sea, create a dream, a dream we can rely on.

We remember Misty birthday parties and public appearances in the 1940s and 1950s. We have apps and websites like MistysHeaven.com. We can see the drill team and Pony

Penning Week with its roundup, swim, auction and carnival attracting thousands of visitors every July.

Through it all, Marguerite's story of a boy and a girl and the pony they loved brings people together, united in their admiration, whether they know Marguerite's name or not. What an enduring, exquisite legacy.

Chapter 33

A Pictorial Life Story of Misty

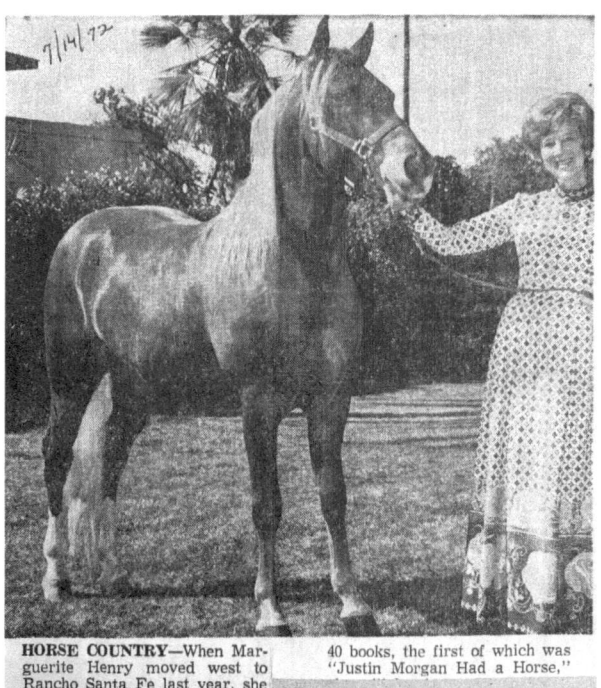

HORSE COUNTRY—When Marguerite Henry moved west to Rancho Santa Fe last year, she brought her award-winning writing skills with her. Author of 40 books, the first of which was "Justin Morgan Had a Horse,"

In 1971, the Henrys sold their beloved Mole Meadow in Wayne, Illinois, and moved to a house in Rancho Santa Fe, California. Marguerite wrote, "On a Pacific hilltop overgrown with daisies we made our home. In no way did the new

Daisy Hill replace our Mole Meadow. We just expanded our hearts to fill both."

I never found out why they left the Midwest, but it was clear why they'd chosen this particular community in California. Not only was the weather great and the view lovely, the area was known for golf and horses. The town just north of San Diego had backyard barns, miles of riding trails winding through the foothills and several golf courses. Although it didn't have a barn, the Henrys' new neighbors had horses. While living at Daisy Hill, Marguerite took up gardening and continued to write.

By this time, Misty was living again on Chincoteague Island at the Beebe Ranch. In *A Pictorial Life Story of Misty*, Marguerite describes joy and sorrow whenever she received a letter from a fan who had visited Misty. One fan wrote about shaking hands with the celebrity pony and remarked, "I didn't know grandmas could be so young!"

Another fan letter shared, "After waiting three years, I finally saw her. Did you know she is 24 years old? Sad to say, you can tell she is getting older. She doesn't look like any of the pictures I saw of her except when she was little. Then she was cute and fuzzy. Now she is fuzzy again."

In 1972, Marguerite received a photo taken of Misty on the pony's twenty-sixth birthday. The then seventy-year-old author reported, "Misty looked just how I remembered her, grazing in a flower-strewn meadow." Three months later, the famous pony died in her sleep.

News of Misty's passing was broadcast around the world. Baltimore's *The Evening Sun* gave the article, "Misty," prime space.

"A million or more children, in this country and abroad, have read the Misty story over the past quarter century. Many were never sure if the story were true or made up, and maybe that didn't matter. What the story brings forth, in its simple and low-key way, is the human capacity for warmth and unselfishness which is a capacity not always predominant and which, to go by the rest of the news, sometimes may not be there at all.

Misty is dead, and that's the least of it. The Misty story lives on, a tiny light in the surrounding gloom."

Ralph Beebe decided to hire a taxidermist to turn Misty's body into a memorial that fans could keep visiting. Charles Oxenham spent a year recreating a stuffed version of the legendary mare. Oxenham reported that it was "nerve-wracking" and "the hardest thing I have ever done."

Fans were divided on whether they thought taxidermy was the right end for Misty, but Marguerite did not like the idea at all. "All my pleas couldn't stop the drive to put Misty on permanent display instead of allowing her a well-earned rest from a lifetime of getting up on her step-stool and shaking hands and giving endless pony rides to endless lines of children and performing in plays and story hours and submitting to smothering hugs."

Some time after the pony's passing, Marguerite received a letter from Paul Merritt. He wanted to make a Misty museum and asked Marguerite to write a book about Misty's life after the events in *Misty of Chincoteague*, *Stormy, Misty's Foal* and *Sea Star*. If she said no, he hoped she would send him pictures that he could display in the museum.

Marguerite wasn't excited about writing another Misty book, but she began setting out photos she could send to Paul. She spread them out on the floor of her library but ran out of space. Marguerite continued laying out pictures in the living room, down the hallway and into her bedroom. Pony photos had taken over her home! In order to avoid trampling the treasured images, Marguerite and Sid booked a room at a nearby inn to stay the night. The next morning, she organized the photos by date. She began thinking about Misty's life and realized it would make a wonderful book.

"Suddenly the idea became intensely real; it took complete possession of me. Misty had lived for 26 years. For all that time she had been a part of my life. The book would be all about her adventures. I didn't mean to let myself in at all, but the paths of our lives had criss-crossed so often—that I couldn't keep it out. The story grew—as natural as Misty herself ... I found myself falling in love with Misty all over again, and it took me almost as long as it takes a mare to foal a colt to complete a story I said I would never, never write at all."

When she was finished, she had created *A Pictorial Life Story of Misty*, published in 1976. The book is full of behind-the-scenes details about the Misty movie, Misty's sheltering in the Beebe's kitchen and her fundraising appearances.

Merritt never finished his museum, but the taxidermied Misty and her daughter Stormy are currently on display at the Museum of Chincoteague Island. When I was there during Pony Penning week, I made a trip to the museum. Like many fans, I had mixed feelings about this display. The stuffed horses are caricatures compared to the photos I'd studied. The taxidermied ponies possess none of their living glory.

As I read the placards near Misty and Stormy, two women entered the room. "Oh no!" one of them gasped, retreating several steps. "I'm not ready for this," she told her friend who stood between her and the stuffed Chincoteague Ponies. I completely understood.

Marguerite never saw the stuffed version of the little mare she loved with all her heart. Although she's gone, Misty is still real in our imagination to those of us who read and cherished her stories. There, she will always be beautiful and young, with shiny golden dapples.

Chapter 34

Book Ideas and Unpublished Stories

"Book ideas have a way of exploding like a barnful of hay in a burning sun—scientists call it spontaneous combustion," Marguerite wrote in a 1967 newsletter. The author had no problem dreaming up her own stories to write. *A Pictorial Life Story of Misty* was not the only book idea pitched to her. She received many book ideas from fans and acquaintances. For example, a marketer presented a book idea about the horse farms of Kentucky. The store this marketer represented was about to open two new stores in Louisville and Lexington, and thought a book by Marguerite would help make the new shops more popular. I thought that was a stellar idea and am disappointed Marguerite didn't go for it.

In 1962, another publisher wrote to suggest Marguerite write a book about horse racing. He mentioned Janus, a horse with an outstanding career. Marguerite's publisher wrote back, "At the present time Marguerite has three or four excellent ideas for books which she wants to write for us, and which we want her to write for us. Marguerite is a meticulous craftsman in her writing and it takes her a good long time to turn out one of her best-selling books. Therefore, we would hate to have her break into the schedule already established, and spend perhaps a year doing a book for another publisher."

The Marguerite Henry archives are full of folders with little snippets of research for books that were never finished. I found one file folder labeled "Snowman," containing a set of three-by-five cards with handwritten notes. Marguerite's artistic cursive scrawled, "I've been looking at the pic of Snowman in my scrapbook and he's the clumsiest (the word "clumsiest" is crossed out) most beautiful lop-eared, flea-bitten gray I … keep thinking of him." Snowman was a rescue horse who became a champion show jumper thanks to the love and friendship of Harry de Leyer. Although Marguerite never wrote this underdog story, Elizabeth Letts did, releasing *The Eighty Dollar Champion* in 2011.

The archives also held folders with Marguerite's own ideas: *Sophia, the Grimy Angel*; *The Two Loves of Alexander*; *Muggs: International Hound*; *Sir Patrick Henry: the Bilingual Dog*; and *Mr. Quackenbush and His Quacker*, about a homeless man and his pet duck.

Marguerite had saved a newspaper clipping of an elderly man in a suit walking his duck. Marguerite's editor didn't think the duck story would work. She wrote, "Children would probably be interested in the pet idea but if they wanted to have a duck in their rooms it would present a problem! Ducks are horribly messy in their toilet habits." As if to soften the blow, she added, "I can see why you wanted to write it and how it would appeal to you, sympathetic creature that you are! The lonely old man would get a hold on your heart strings."

I love that Marguerite wanted to take on the topics of poverty and homelessness to show children there's more to life than pony parties, birthday cake and happy endings. Who better to engage children with the fact that sometimes life is really hard, unfair even, than a trusted author friend like Marguerite? The idea was ahead of its time.

Although she had to put many ideas to the side, Marguerite kept writing.

One file in the archives contains a whole unpublished book titled *Mini-Horses*. I read it, studied the photographs, then Googled photographer Tom Nebbia, whose name was on the cover with Marguerite's. It turned out he was quite famous too. His photography had appeared in *National Geographic* magazine, and he had snapped portraits of U.S. presidents. Why wasn't this almost-finished book by such a famous writer and photographer published? The answer was complicated. The book had been backed by *Reading Rainbow Gazette*, but they had never secured a publisher. The manuscript was eventually returned to Marguerite, unpublished.

I shot an iPhone video of the manuscript, thinking about the many Marguerite Henry fans who would be delighted to see the photos of Miniature Horses and read Marguerite's stories about them. I wondered if the University of Minnesota had ever considered publishing it. That led me to sad news: Marguerite Henry had instructed the University of Minnesota not to publish any unpublished work or allow the publication or adaptation of her books. The only way to see her unpublished stories is by investigating the archive at the University of Minnesota.

Chapter 35

Marguerite's Twilight

> **INTER-OFFICE MEMORANDUM** — RIVERSIDE CITY COLLEGE
>
> TO: Marguerite Henry DATE: November 1, 1980
> SUBJECT: Thanks
>
> Thank you for enriching my children's lives (and indeed, that of my whole family) through the years. Surely nothing is more rewarding than children and horses are.
>
> Thank you, too, for what you have meant to my children's literature classes in college. What a triumphant life yours is — bringing so much joy to others through your artistry.
>
> Sincerely,
> Dina Stallings
> SIGNED
>
> *This note washes away all the worry. M.H.*

Bonnie Shields illustrated what would be Marguerite's last book, *Brown Sunshine of Sawdust Valley*. It's the story of a girl who yearned for a horse but wound up with a baby mule.

Bonnie formed a friendship with Marguerite as they collaborated on Marguerite's mule book. She would sometimes stay at the Henrys' in California. The trio of Bonnie, Sidney and Marguerite would have indoor picnics and spend time by the pool. Bonnie got to see Marguerite reading and saving fan mail. The writer's office was an ever-changing collage of art projects and photos from fans across the country. Marguerite was getting too old to visit schools and libraries, but she sometimes spoke to classes via telephone, and she did her best to reply to every letter she received.

Bonnie also got to see the aging couple together. She described Sidney as "a real sweet and intelligent man and Marguerite's first and best fan. Theirs was a love story as far as I could see." Marguerite stopped working for about three years when Sidney became ill. He was eight years older than Marguerite and died in 1987. His ashes were scattered at sea.

"When he died, she shut down for a while, but working on our book was her escape, and when she felt ready, we picked it up seriously. I have a precious little card framed in my studio from her saying she was in her writing room and working on *Brown Sunshine*—and she was HAPPY!"

In addition to *Brown Sunshine*, Marguerite began working on a tribute to Sidney in the form of her own autobiography. She had never wanted to write about herself, but at the urging of her editor, Joyce Nakamura, she began to reconsider.

"My mind recoiled at the bumptiousness of writing a book about oneself. But there was something about Ms. Nakamura's insistence that I felt I was being directed by a Higher Source. My writing began to leap over all my objections, for to my joy, it became Sid's story. We were together again! He, through God, was directing my course as he had done all of his life. I wrote the piece to him ... the writing made me whole again."

In 1988's *Something About the Author* Marguerite wrote, "In 1987 Sidney Crocker Henry died. But no one has ever died less. He is still watching over Misty's world. What stronger proof than this? Cloudy (Misty's first grandson) and Stormy (Misty's last daughter) are getting along in years. They needed a roof over their heads to shut out the burning sun and deflect the stinging botflies and mosquitoes. Sid must have sensed such problems might arise for he left in his will money to build that roof to shade Misty's children. Life is nice and round, isn't it? As Grandma Beebe, the comforter, said to me when Grandpa Beebe died, 'No one ever dies, not a person or even a single pony. Nothing dies as long as there is the memory to enfold it and a heart to love it.'"

Once the autobiography was complete, Marguerite began writing *Misty's Twilight*. It is the tale of Sandy Price, a doctor and single mother from Florida, who hitched an empty horse trailer to her truck and set off to Chincoteague with her children. The main character in the story adored Misty as a girl, and wanted to show her children the island ponies and bring one home. After watching the swim and going to the auction, the Price family returned home with not one Chincoteague pony, but FIVE! Three of the ponies were foals and one was a pregnant mare named Sunshine. Two years later, Misty's Twilight was born. In the book published in 1992, this pony is a prodigy who excelled in cutting, a western event where a single cow is separated from a group of cows; jumping; and later dressage.

The story seemed like a wonderful dream and an excellent way to end the Misty stories. But it turns out Misty's Twilight had been a real pony!

On September 1, 1996, *Brown Sunshine of Sawdust Valley* was published, Marguerite's final work. It had been almost eighteen years in the making. A little over a year later, when she was ninety-five, Marguerite began having strokes. On November 16, 1997, Marguerite died at home with her poodle, Patrick Henry, at her side. A niece and nephew scattered her ashes at sea; Marguerite and Sidney were together again.

Marguerite had arranged for her home to be donated to a hospital foundation. Her writings were left to the University of Minnesota. As her books continue to sell, the money pays for a children's literature professor position, the Sidney and Marguerite Henry Professor of Children's and Young Adult Literature. Marek Oziewicz has the position currently. Marek is not horse-obsessed, but his job exists because of Marguerite Henry's books. He has a lot of respect for Marguerite: "I can't think of any author who writes about horses with such dedication. Marguerite was one of the voices who advocated for horses specifically, and animals in general, as creatures we need to be good to. Relating to a horse makes us better people."

Ralph Waldo Emerson defined success as follows: "To laugh often and much: To win the respect of intelligent people and the affection of children, to earn the appreciation of honest critics and endure the betrayal of false friends; to appreciate beauty, to find the best in others, to leave the world a bit better whether by a healthy child, a garden patch, or a redeemed social condition; to know even one life has breathed easier because you lived. This is to have succeeded."

Marguerite Henry lived such a life, winning the affection of children and leaving the world better through her timeless books. A professor once wrote to her, "Thank you for enriching my children's lives (and indeed, that of my whole family) through the years. Surely nothing is more rewarding than children and horses are. Thank you, too, for what you have meant to my children's literature classes in college. What a triumphant life yours is—bringing so much joy to others through your artistry."

Beneath the note Marguerite had written, "This note washes away all the work."

Following Marguerite's death, a news reporter wrote, "No other individual of our day has had a greater impact on Chincoteague than this woman who loved children, and horses."

A successful and triumphant life indeed.

Chapter 36

Marguerite's Kindness

In 1946, Marguerite stayed at Miss Molly's Inn on Chincoteague as she researched for *Misty*. She found a live seahorse near the beach and scooped it into a glass of water, which she placed by the window of her room. When she awoke the next morning, the white curtains were covered in baby seahorses, which had burst from their father's pouch during the night. In a 1983 note to the bed and breakfast,

Marguerite wrote, "In embarrassment and haste I gathered father and children up and returned them to the sea. And that is why the finial to the book of Misty is decorated with a sketch of a seahorse." Marguerite was world-famous and had achieved the highest award in her field. Yet she was not too proud to share her awkward moments. This was just one part of her personality that made her special.

Marguerite dedicated herself to returning fan mail, publishing a newsletter, making appearances at schools and libraries and writing stories to delight us, even into her nineties. She was passionate, just like the workhorse in her book *5 O 'clock Charlie*. In that story, a life of retirement in a lonely field did not suit the aged cart horse, so he leaped a fence and trotted into town where he saw his old friends and rang a bell daily at five o'clock. Charlie needed purpose and longed for connection, and so did Marguerite. She was working on her manuscript about Patrick Henry, her poodle, when she died. She never retired.

One of the Marguerite Henry files contained a peculiar sticky note from an editor. It had been cut and repositioned so an original section was no longer visible. The surviving part read, "I have done my best to live up to your expectations and trust ... I have handled this with as much tenderness and pride as one would a newborn filly, or a brand new baby sister! Thank you for taking me along (for the ride!)!" Marguerite had jotted a comment on the side: "I expurgated the materials. It was too generous of praise." Marguerite had cut up the note.

She also was not too proud (nor busy) to volunteer. During the 1950s, Marguerite headed to a local hospital one day a week. She had just received the Newbery Medal, yet her busy schedule did not keep her from visiting people, connecting with them in a time of pain. Maybe she remembered the days when she had been sick as a child and wanted to help others connect to books as she had.

As of 1979, Marguerite had sold over thirteen million copies of her books. I tried finding the current statistic for how many books she has sold, but publishers keep that information private. In that same year, she wrote a letter to a little girl empathizing with her yearning for a horse: "I know EXACTLY how you feel about looking at people up on a horse. They look so happy at being there that you yourself want to crawl under a rock and cry. For many years—in fact all of my school years—I lived without a horse. It wasn't until I was completely grown up and could afford a horse of my own that I was able to buy a fine black Morgan. He was worth all the waiting and longing."

No matter her age or how famous she became, Marguerite remained, in her heart, a girl who dreamed of and lived for horses. She knew just the right things to say to those of us who were horseless, and the stories she penned were love letters to an animal, and to us.

In 2022, Susan stayed in the room at Miss Molly's Inn where Marguerite wrote Misty in 1946.

Chapter 37

Getting Lost While the Artwork Was Being Found

Two weeks after Pony Penning, I was back at the archives at the University of Minnesota. I put headphones on like a DJ in a club to listen to a radio interview from 1951. The interview was a promotion for the book *Album of Horses*. I listened to the whole recording while furiously typing a transcript of the conversation. I'm pretty sure I had a smile on my face the whole time.

The host of the show introduced Marguerite and said, "Since you started to write about horses, I always think of you with perhaps a pony trailing behind or a couple of horses over in the next field."

"I like to be thought of in that way." Marguerite's voice was honey sweet.

Wesley Dennis teased her about Misty getting spoiled with too many treats and Marguerite rose to the pony's defense. She said it was the pony's "long hair that makes her look fat. And when she's wet and we give her a bath, she looks sleek as a seal."

Through their lighthearted banter, I sensed they enjoyed working with each other very much. Marguerite compared herself to a workhorse who goes along steadily, and she described Wesley as a fleet Thoroughbred. She said they weren't a matched team, like two Clydesdales, but their strengths worked together, and they both made it to the finish line.

I'd seen some of Wesley Dennis's art at a special exhibit, but I hoped to see some of his sketches and horse illustrations up close. I reserved a box at the archives, but when I arrived, the librarians couldn't find it. Not knowing what else to do, I began reviewing more folders of fan mail to Marguerite.

I found a January 1995 letter from a reading teacher stating, "My fifth and sixth grade girls and boys thoroughly enjoyed your book *Misty of Chincoteague*. We wanted to write to let you know your popularity is not diminished since your heyday of the 50's and 60's [sic]."

Handwritten notes from a beginner's large, plain print to artful teachers' script said much the same: I read your book, I like this part, I have a question, and I hope you'll write back. She almost always did. She even formed lasting friendships with some, becoming penpals for life.

As a teacher, I knew the pressure of encouraging, challenging and ultimately loving my students. Marguerite loved, befriended and empathized with thousands of children around the world for over sixty years. Although she never had a child of her own, Marguerite possessed a motherly, and later grandmotherly affection and concern for her fans.

She once wrote about the upside down nature of her life. In the 1930s, most young women spent their early years caring for their children, and when the little ones had grown, mothers would start work outside the home. "To Sid's and my surprise we had no chick or child of our own even though we both came from large families. So I spent my young married years in the lively pursuit of word-chasing." She went on to say in her "ungrandmotherly" years she was taking care of the children she never had—her young readers who wrote her letters with "monstrous problems," sharing their sadness at the loss of a pet, divorcing parents, and even thoughts of suicide. If a child expressed such dark thoughts to her, phone calls were made. She truly loved people and was committed to them. She imparted that gift to her readers.

Even after her death, the fan mail kept coming. Lee Galda, the first Sidney and Marguerite Henry Professor of Children's and Young Adult Literature at the University of Minnesota, was responsible for crafting a response letter for fans who wrote to Marguerite, unaware she had passed away. Although she was a writer and professor, Lee said writing that letter was one of the hardest things she's ever had to do.

I continued flipping through papers, scanning the messages from decades earlier. Stationery with muted golds and greens of a palomino in a sea of prairie grass snagged my attention. I'd had that same paper when I was a girl! A few minutes later, I found a letter on lined notebook paper. The careful cursive looked almost exactly like my little-girl penmanship.

Next I felt the bumps of a Braille letter. Alongside it was a note to tell Marguerite that her response had been transcribed into Braille. I thought how cool it was that Marguerite valued connecting with all of her readers. She cared about inclusion and diversity. *Misty of Chincoteague* and *Brighty of the Grand Canyon* were both made into Braille books. *A Pictorial Life Story* of Misty reports that Misty gave one last ride before going back to Chincoteague; that rider was a blind girl. In her short educational film, *Story of a Book*, a Black girl and an Asian boy paged through books, and one of the child narrators spoke with a distinct southern accent. In *Black Gold*, she wrote about the 1924 Kentucky Derby winner, bred and owned by a woman of the Osage Nation. Marguerite wanted to elevate untold stories and hoped all of her fans would feel represented. In many ways, she was ahead of the times.

CHAPTER 38

MARGUERITE, MY MUSE

I was so lost in the fan mail that I was surprised when the archive curator interrupted me. She apologized that the Wesley Dennis artwork was taking so long to find and offered to take me on a tour of the archives. I agreed right away.

An elevator lowered us into the literary cavern the size of two football fields. We walked through a tunnel designed to keep the artifacts at the perfect temperature and humidity so they would last as long as possible. Metal shelves towered floor to ceiling in the vast cavern, some rising fifteen shelves high. Specially trained employees use a cherry picker to retrieve materials for researchers.

"The author Pam Muñoz Ryan wrote a letter to Marguerite Henry when she was a kid," the curator said as we ambled aisle after aisle. "She looked for it when she was here once." I had read Pam's book *Esperanza Rising*. Did Marguerite inspire Pam to be a writer too? I later emailed her to ask. I didn't get to write Marguerite, but because of Marguerite, I had the courage to write another beloved children's author. She replied that her horse books *Paint the Wind* and *Riding Freedom* were a nod to *King of the Wind*.

I recalled my regret at never writing to Marguerite Henry, despite having her address tucked away in my desk drawer for years. But it hit me then: it didn't matter. I had not lost an opportunity to get to know my favorite author. In fact, I had gotten to know her much more than I would have after a single letter. I had been on a personal mission to find Marguerite, and now I could share that story and connect with many fans and readers who still love her. She brought sweet, uplifting stories into the world, and I believe with all my heart the world still needs sweet, uplifting stories.

One fan letter said exactly what I was thinking: "I was one of those children you wrote for in the past. I think that loving and caring for animals develops traits in a child's character of kindness and understanding for all life on this Earth. For me, as I am sure it is with many others, your stories live past a fleeting fascination of youth and become an integral part of one's being."

Marguerite's stories had become a part of my being!

I will never be the kind of writer Marguerite was, but by knowing who she was, perhaps I can be a little more like her. I've started keeping a file folder system like she did. I've been digging into research with enthusiasm, just like Marguerite's. And perhaps a little of her kindness and warmth have become a part of me too. I haven't bought a pinto Chincoteague Pony for my very own, but my real life story with the real ponies, is still being written.

During my research, I made incredible acquaintances, and met her in-real-life friends. I met Ed Richardson, the man who, as a little boy, rode Misty after school in the 1950s. I spoke with Matt, the man behind MistysHeaven.com who wants to have an online space for Misty fans to see pictures of Misty's family that makes them happy. I met Kendy, the retired librarian committed to preserving the Misty line of

Chincoteague ponies. I befriended Amanda and Rebekah of the International Chincoteague Pony Registry and Association, who are trying to preserve and protect bloodlines while promoting the breed. And I'd connected to a whole community of pony-lovers and readers who still love Marguerite's stories.

While searching for Marguerite's writing history, I noticed her word play and hand-written notes. I studied both her research and writing techniques and can now try to write like she did. I feel like the fan who wrote to her October 20, 1993: "I am a writer too and have so much to learn from craftsmen like you. Maybe by the time I'm ninety I'll have a portion of your skill!" Like this letter writer, I'm still learning.

I uncovered behind-the-scenes stories about Marguerite and Misty that never made it into her fifty-nine books from *Auno and Tauno* to *Brown Sunshine*. There were so many stories, it would take many books like this one to describe them all.

Although I never dropped a letter addressed to Marguerite in a mailbox, I "met" Marguerite again and again while writing this book. Instead of feeling sad that I'd missed out, I realized I need to celebrate what Marguerite had given me: adventure, friendship, pony joy, and an island haven. Pony Penning is months away at the time of this writing, but I almost can't wait to return. I'm sure I'll meet old and new friends, and I'll definitely bring stronger mosquito spray.

This letter from a fan captured the spirit of everything that Marguerite Henry meant to me as a child and still means to me today: "Mrs. Henry, your name is synonymous with love, beauty, passion, integrity and courage. I am so grateful to God for your books; and to you for responding in the concreteness of the literature you have taken the time to write ... I have felt many, many things while reading your literature, but never sorry, bored or disappointed. Always I feel moved to do greater things in my life."

I never met her, nor sent her a letter, but I found Marguerite, my muse, and so much more.

If Marguerite were still alive today, I would find some pretty horse stationery and write a thank you to her. It would go like this:

Dear Marguerite,

I have been a fan of yours for as long as I can remember. Thank you for bringing so much joy into my life through the pages of Misty of Chincoteague, and really all of your books. I feel as though we are kindred spirits, as I love libraries too. In fact, I grew up reading and borrowing your horse books from the Gail Borden Public Library where you used to go to research. Small world. Your books have inspired me to be a lifelong reader, and for that I am grateful.

Also, you and I have something in common: Wayne! I learned how to ride on a borrowed Quarter Horse named Jim Dandy. He was an old field hunter owned by my parents' friend Cindy, who lived on Dunham Road. I'll never forget going for a swim with Jim, the bright chestnut, in the quarry not far from Mole Meadow. When I finally got the horse of my dreams, DC, in my twenties, I showed him and won Reserve Champion at a hunter/jumper show held across the street from what was then called Dunham Woods, right down the street from your Mole Meadow home.

I owned and loved DC for sixteen years. When he died, I was horseless for several years. Then I found my handsome Knight. Literally. My dark bay Thoroughbred's name is Tiz a Knight, sired by the legendary Tiznow, who is the only horse to have won the Breeders' Cup Classic twice.

Words can't describe how much I love Knight and what a true friend he has been to me in the last eight years we've been together. I want to be a better horsewoman with each passing day so that I do right by Knight always.

Although I'm an adult, I still want to grow up to be like you. I want your A++ creativity, your tireless work ethic, and unwavering optimism. Thank you for welcoming us, your readers, into the world of horses, especially when we had no way to get to a farm or a barn to know and love them firsthand. You made sure all of your fans felt like Misty belonged to them just as we belonged to her and to each other. Oh how I wish your generous spirit were more dominant in the horse world of today.

Because of you, Marguerite, I have befriended many fellow horse and pony lovers I would have never met were it not for the story of a pretty pinto who once roamed an island. Thank you, Marguerite. I'm so grateful for all you've taught me and for who you are.

Sincerely,
Your Number One Fan,
Susan (& Knight)

Epilogue

In case you were wondering if I ever got to view the Wesley Dennis art, the answer is yes.

When the boxes arrived, I felt like I was doing the opposite of making lasagna. When I lifted off the box lid, there were alternating layers of art and archival papers instead of pasta and cheese. I would lift off a paper and see a sketch. Place the sketch on the table, lift off another archival paper, and there would be another drawing. It was so fun.

If you want to see Wesley Dennis art too, all you have to do is go to your library and ask to see any books by Marguerite Henry that are illustrated by Wesley Dennis, or books that he wrote (may I suggest *Flip*?). You will be glad you took the time to find his drawings, I guarantee it.

And there's one last thing I *have* to share.

As you know, I never met Marguerite, and never attended one of her book signings.

However, when I started researching to write *Marguerite, Misty and Me*, I found an autographed copy of *Misty* for sale online. I had to buy it.

Don't you think it was meant to be?

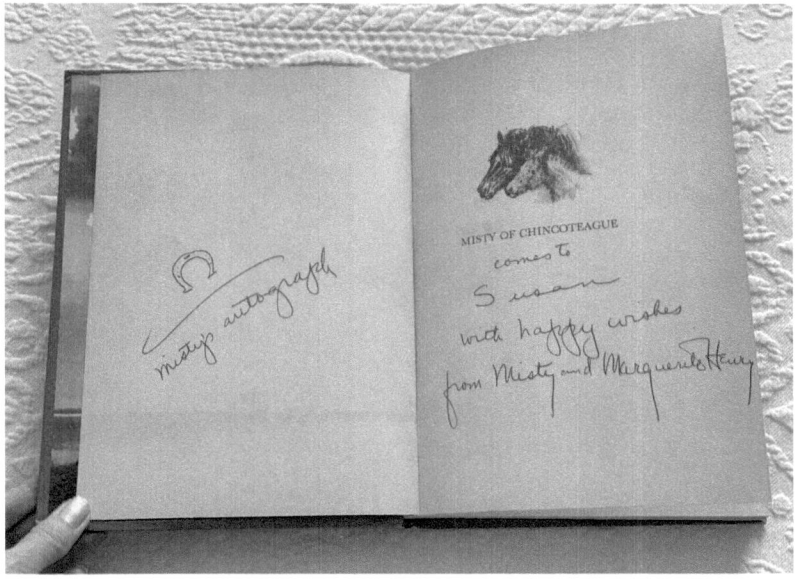

TIMELINE OF MARGUERITE HENRY'S LIFE

1902	Marguerite Anna is born on April 13 in Milwaukee, Wisconsin, to Louis and Anna Breithaupt.
1913	Sells her first story "Hide and Seek in Autumn Leaves" to *The Delineator* magazine.
1920	Graduates from Riverside High School. Held leadership roles in the yearbook, drama, and Bible study clubs.
1922	Graduates from college with a degree in journalism. Meets Sidney Crocker Henry at a fishing camp in Minocqua, Wisconsin.
1923	Marries Sidney May 5 and moves to Chicago.
1940	Publishes two children's picture books *Dilly Dally Sally* and *Auno and Tauno: a Story of Finland*.
1945	Purchases property in Wayne, Illinois, which became Mole Meadow, publishes *Justin Morgan Had a Horse*.
1946	Visits Chincoteague Island to see the wild ponies swim, buys Misty from Grandpa Beebe.
1947	Publishes *Misty of Chincoteague* which is awarded a Newbery Honor.
1948	Publishes *King of the Wind* which is awarded the Newbery Medal in 1949.
1961	*Misty of Chincoteague* movie is released, filmed on location in Chincoteague, Virginia.
1962	Publishes *Stormy, Misty's Foal*.
1996	Publishes last book *Brown Sunshine of Sawdust Valley*.
1997	Dies at home November 26 in Rancho Santa Fe, California at age 95.

TIMELINE OF WORLD EVENTS

1902	First Rose Bowl football game occurrs in Pasadena, CA. Michigan beats Stanford 49-0.
1914	World War I begins with conflict between the Allies and Central Powers in Europe.
1918	World War I ends with an agreement of peace between Germany and the Allies.
1920	19th Amendment passes giving women the right to vote.
1923	Roy and Walt Disney start up The Walt Disney Company.
1929	The Wall Street stock market crash marks the beginning of the Great Depression.
1932	Amelia Earhart becomes the first woman to make a nonstop solo transatlantic flight.
1938	Seabiscuit is voted American Horse of the Year.
1939	World War II begins with conflict between the Allies and Axis powers.
1941	Marvel Comics introduces superhero Captain America.
1945	World War II ends with the German and Japanese surrender to the Allies.
1947	Jackie Robinson becomes the first African American to play in Major League Baseball.
1963	Martin Luther King, Jr. delivers "I Have a Dream" speech in Washington D.C.
1969	Apollo 11 lands on the moon, and Neil Armstrong walks on its surface.
1973	Secretariat wins horse racing's Triple Crown.
1997	Google.com is registered as a domain name.

INTERVIEW WITH THE AUTHOR

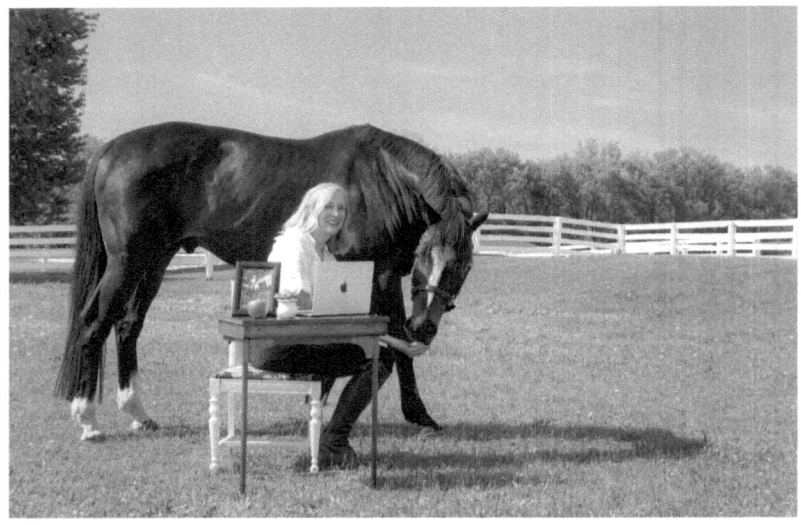

Question: What were some of the surprising facts you learned about Marguerite Henry and the pony Misty?

Susan Friedland: I was surprised to learn that Marguerite Henry launched her own writing career by walking into a publisher's office, asking for a writing assignment, and telling the editor that if he didn't like what she wrote, they wouldn't have to pay her. That was a bold move, especially for a woman in 1923. Think of it: just three years earlier, women got the right to vote in the U.S. thanks to the 19th Amendment. I learned she was a go-getter and extremely confident. I don't know that I would have had her moxie. Regarding Misty, I didn't realize she was such a celebrity, with themed merchandise like puzzles and squeaky toys made in her image. I also learned about her annual birthday parties and her appearance at the American Library Association convention in 1949.

Q: Can you share your writing process? Where did you write? How long did the book take to research, write and edit?

SF: Sure. It was a long and crazy process. I started my initial research in 2019 and the "older reader" copy of *Marguerite, Misty and Me* was published in 2023. I felt like I didn't know what I was doing half the time. I started with a few questions I wanted to discover the answers to such as "How did Marguerite Henry get to be such a good writer?" and "What was Misty like as a riding pony?" The more cool information I found out, the more questions I had. I wrote in my office most of the time, which is a spare bedroom with a desk looking out the window. Occasionally, I would go to a coffee shop.

Q: Were there any challenges you encountered while writing this book? How did you overcome them?

SF: I had so many wonderful facts about Marguerite and Misty. It was hard to organize the book into a cohesive whole. I took poster paper and made graphic organizers like a circle map, tree map, and lots of lists. I used the same graphic organizers I taught my sixth and seventh grade students to use to help their writing.

Another challenge I faced was how to organize and cite my sources. My developmental editor pointed out that since this book is technically a memoir, I didn't have to cite sources to show where I found the information in this book. However, I thought back to teaching my middle school students how important is is to keep track of where you find information, making sure your sources are credible (because as you know, just because you read it online doesn't mean it's true). I thought it was important to show my sources. Who knows? Maybe one of my readers will pick up the baton and dig even further into research about Chincoteague Ponies or one of their favorite topics. I hope they can use my example as somewhat of a template. Also, if you have dozens of sources, you'll need a citation management system. I used the app PaperPile, and it was amazing.

Q: What messages do you want readers to walk away with from this book?

SF: I hope readers will try riding a horse at least once! And I definitely hope they will read some of Marguerite Henry's books. But also, I think it's important (and fun) to practice being curious and follow that curiosity. Research is not boring, and you can't rely on just Google and the internet to teach you things. Sometimes you need to go to a place and talk to locals. I hope readers will talk to people—especially older folks, and ask them questions. Ultimately, this is a story about following your dream. Marguerite did, and I did too.

Q: Is there a certain scene from your writing journey or book research when you wish you the reader had been right there next to you?

SF: Yes! I wish I my readers could have joined me in a kayak for the Chincoteague Pony swim! The excitement of all the other kayakers and people on boats was intense. The ponies are so beautiful, and *Misty* is such a sweet story, and the swim is exactly like the storybook. It's hard to explain the awesomeness.

Q: What do you like about being an author, and what advice do you have for aspiring writers?

SF: Writing can be hard and lonely. When I get stuck on a tricky passage or find it challenging to smooth out a sentence, I think about the future readers who might smile or be inspired by the information I'm sharing. It is heartwarming to have people I've never met in real life send me messages about how much ***Marguerite, Misty and Me*** meant to them and how they want to go back and reread their childhood horse books by Marguerite.

I think writing is a wonderful activity—it's essentially free, you can learn a ton, and you can meet like-minded fellow writers (and readers) who become friends. If you've ever contemplated writing a book, I say, "Go for it!" Write the book you want to read. That's what I did. And don't let the fact that you're young stop you. Marguerite was just a girl when her first writing was published. But remember, writing is like riding a horse, or playing a sport or musical instrument, really. In order to be good, you have to practice. I've written a lot of boring or too-long sentences. You have to start somewhere.

Also, you can be like Marguerite and join your school's yearbook staff, a literary club or a drama club. If your school doesn't have one of those types of clubs, ask a teacher or your principal to help you get one started. If you're horse-crazy like me, you could ask to start an equestrian club.

Whatever you do, keep on reading and writing!

Notes

Here's a list of the archival collections I used to research, along with their abbreviations. Below that you will see the sources I used by chapter. Some of them I found via a Google search, but many were records and documents I needed to see in person because they are not online. There is a wealth of information in the world that is never digitized. I hope you will research in the offline world too.

(ALA) American Library Association Archives
University of Illinois
(GRHC) Grand Rapids History Center
Grand Rapids, Michigan
(HFP) Harvey Family Papers, Newberry Library
Chicago, Illinois
(MCHS) Milwaukee County Historical Society
Milwaukee, Wisconsin
(MHC) Marguerite Henry Collection, Kerlan Collection of Children's Literature

University of Minnesota

(MHP) Marguerite Henry Papers, DuPage County Historical Museum

Wheaton, Illinois

(RMC) Rand McNally Collection, Newberry Library

Chicago, Illinois

(SCPL) St. Charles Public Library

St. Charles, Illinois

CHAPTER 1: WILD, SWIMMING PONIES

Ask your parents to take you to Chincoteague Island in July for Pony Penning Week. If they say yes, you might want to save your money and start a pony fund. You can thank me later!

CHAPTER 2: THE HORSE PROBLEM

If you haven't read the books I mention in this chapter, you're missing out. Ask your librarian to find *King of the Wind*, *Brighty of the Grand Canyon* and *Misty of Chincoteague* for you. Trust me, they'd love to help. If horses aren't your thing, but you love meerkats or lacrosse or coding or something else totally different, still ask your librarian to help you find books on what you love.

CHAPTER 3: POPULAR PONY BOOKS

Lost dozens of their personal herd: "The True Tale of Misty, Stormy, and Maybe the Worst Nor'easter of Them All - Misty of Chincoteague." *Secrets of the Eastern Shore*, Feb 19, 2015.

reestablish the herds over on Assateague Island: *Letter to Doris Sutherland*. April 4, 1962. MHC Box 22.

CHAPTER 4: WHEN INSPIRATION STRIKES

I remember it like yesterday": Laura Murry Interview, June 14, 2021.

CHAPTER 5: THE IDEA GALLOPS AWAY WITH ME

When I wrote the original version of *Marguerite, Misty and Me*, I only knew of the *Sunset* magazine article about Brighty that gave Marguerite the idea to travel to the Grand Canyon and bring the burro's tale to life. A reader named Lauren Hoeffer who is as obsessed with Brighty as I am with Misty had a digital copy of the 1922 magazine. I got to read the whole thing, and it was all great until the end! In Marguerite's book based on facts she left out a grisly one. When Brighty was an old, old burro, some people got lost in the Grand

Canyon. They were starving and they ate Brighty. Ugh! But if you travel to the Grand Canyon today, in the visitor's center there is a lovely bronze sculpture in honor of the little donkey. So in Marguerite's book and in the visitor's center, Brighty lives on.

CHAPTER 6: THE NEWBERY MEDAL AND OTHER AWARDS

as modest as Marguerite Henry!": Alberita R. Semrad, "Marguerite Henry, Newbery Medal Winner." *Publishers' Weekly*, March 26, 1949.

well enough to buy it": Melinda Miller. Rand McNally & Company Press Release. February 18, 1949. MHP.

I read in disbelief": Marguerite Henry. *A Pictorial Life Story of Misty*. Rand McNally 1976.

department store Herpolsheimer's: "Librarians Plan Meet." *The Grand Rapids Press* October 26, 1949.

a letterhead and a wish": Marguerite Henry, "Newbery Acceptance Paper." *The Horn Book Magazine*, January-February 1950.

I accept the Newbery Medal": Ibid.

taken by *The Grand Rapids Press*: Misty photo taken at the banquet hall, *The Grand Rapids Press*. GRHC.

children who crowded the store": Alberita R. Semrad,

"Marguerite Henry, Newbery Medal Winner." *Publishers' Weekly*, March 26, 1949.

The Little Fellow has just gone into a Spanish edition": Gertrude B. Jupp, "My Little Sister Marguerite Henry." *Horn Book Magazine*, January-February 1950.

there is little danger that they will ever go to her head": Ibid.

CHAPTER 7: THE HANDS-OFF HORSE

Bonnie was also a bucker and a bolter." Mary, "Misty, the Horse That Belongs to Every Child." *The Chicago Tribune*, October 9, 1977.

small words in a small voice: Letter to Bay Shore Union Free School District. MHC September 1993. Box 8 Folder 15.

CHAPTER 8: MARGUERITE FROM MILWAUKEE

who could glide without wings: Marguerite Henry, *Junior Book of Authors*. Edited by Stanley J. Kunitz and Howard Haycraft. 2nd ed. H. W. Wilson Company, 1951.

Editors could be wrong, but not Gertrude": Ibid.

printer's ink got into my blood: *The Daily Journal*. "Her

Love of Printed Word Is Shared with the Young," September 9, 1988.

picked it up very gingerly: Marguerite Henry, Rough Draft of *Something About the Author* MHC Box 2 Folder 11.

They were working too: Ibid.

The more you read, the better you write. —Anonymous: Ibid.

dog's long tongue to lap it up. Ibid.

***The Delineator* July and August 1914:** accessed from the University of Pennsylvania's online archives https://onlinebooks.library.upenn.edu/webbin/serial?id=delineator.

"My hobby is words": Rough Draft of *Something About the Author* MHC Box 2 Folder 11.

rheumatic fever from the ages 10-12: 1968 MH Interview on YouTube https://www.youtube.com/watch?v=gEJIb6JHpoE&t=189.

"signs on the gates of heaven": Rough Draft of *Something About the Author* MHC Box 2 Folder 11.

a public swimming pool: Bobby Tanzilo, "Urban Spelunking: Diving into the History of Milwaukee's Natatoria." *On Milwaukee.* January 16, 2018. https://onmilwaukee.com/articles/milwaukee-natatoriums.

***The Mercury*:** Milwaukee County Historical Society. *The Mercury* 1917-1920 yearbooks.

never published: Charles , "Horse Lovers' 'Dear Abby'": *Los Angeles Times*, November 11, 1979.
as determined by the English faculty.": Milwaukee County Historical Society. *The Echo*: 1921 yearbook.
the silken swish of super-stylish clothes": Milwaukee County Historical Society. *The Echo*: 1922 yearbook.

CHAPTER 9: LOVE IN A PINE FOREST

even their future dreams.": David R. Collins, *Write a Book for Me: The Story of Marguerite Henry* Morgan Reynolds Incorporated,1999.
meet Marguerite's parents: Ibid.
fashionable flapper: *The Milwaukee Journal*, engagement notice April 29, 1923.
white sweetpeas and sweetheart roses.": "Brilliant Wedding of Sidney C. Henry and Miss Breithaupt," *The Sheboygan Press Telegram* (Sheboygan, WI), 9 May 1923, Wed, p. 6.
Hotel Astor in downtown Milwaukee: Bobby Tanzilo, "Urban Spelunking: The Astor Hotel." *On Milwaukee*, April 13, 2021, https://onmilwaukee.com/articles/astor-on-the-lake.

CHAPTER 10: A JOURNALIST'S JOURNEY

all I could do was write": Kathleen Burns, "Meet DuPage Author Marguerite Henry, and Her 'Misty.'" *The Chicago Tribune*, November 25, 1968.

at the time of construction: "American Furniture Mart." *Chicagology*, https://chicagology.com/skyscrapers/skyscrapers001/.

"I could take notes!": Marguerite Henry, "Adventures of a Ghost Writer." *Writer's Digest*, Oct. 1935.

Boiling things down ever since": Kathleen Burns, "Meet DuPage Author Marguerite Henry, and Her 'Misty.'" *The Chicago Tribune*, November 25, 1968.

honeymoon lamp squabble with Sidney: Marguerite Henry. "Ornamental Lamps, Well Placed Add Beauty and Restfulness." *Photoplay*, May 1925.

you don't have to be in a certain mood: Marguerite Henry, "Adventures of a Ghost Writer." *Writer's Digest*, Oct. 1935.

she'd heard no's before: Marguerite Henry. *Something About the Author*. 1988. MHP.

'Turning Points in the Lives of Famous Men.'": Melinda Miller. Rand McNally & Company Press Release. February 18, 1949. Marguerite Henry Papers, DuPage County Historical Museum.

I like animals": Marguerite Henry, *Dear Marguerite Henry*. Ranch McNally & Company, 1969 p. 206.

CHAPTER 11: FROM PRETZEL CITY TO A HORSE COMMUNITY

an illustrator who lived nearby: Gertrude B. Jupp, "My Little Sister Marguerite Henry." *Horn Book Magazine*, January-February 1950.

pulls them in a sleigh under the northern lights: Henry, Marguerite, and Gladys Rourke Blackwood. *Auno and Tauno: A Story of Finland*. Albert Whitman & Co., 1940.

young things human or otherwise: Gertrude B. Jupp, "My Little Sister Marguerite Henry." *Horn Book Magazine*, January-February 1950.

***Auno and Tauno*:** Henry, Marguerite, and Gladys Rourke Blackwood. *Auno and Tauno: A Story of Finland*. Albert Whitman & Co., 1940.

Dilly Dally Sally: Henry, Marguerite, and Gladys Rourke Blackwood. *Dilly Dally Sally*. Saalfield Pub. Co., 1940.

Geraldine Belinda: Henry, Marguerite. *Geraldine Belinda*. Platt & Munk Co. 1942.

Their First Igloo: True, Barbara and Marguerite Henry. *Their First Igloo*. Albert Whitman & Co. 19.

paid for it or not": Marguerite Henry. *The Illustrated Mar-*

guerite Henry: With Wesley Dennis, Robert Lougheed, Lynd Ward, and Rich Rudish*. Rand McNally, 1980

drawings on paper are owned by collectors today: Abby Beall, "Wesley Dennis." *The Art of Wesley Dennis*, http://wesleydennis.com/

CHAPTER 12: THE REAL MISTY PONY

Misty of Chincoteague was born:" Marguerite Henry speech. "*Who Carry Umbrellas*" American Library Association, 1961.

To suck in lungsful of air": Marguerite Henry, *Dear Marguerite Henry*. Rand McNally & Co., 1969.

silky as milkweed floss: Mary Daniels, "Misty, the Horse That Belongs to Every Child." *The Chicago Tribune*, October 9, 1977.

I'd be there for her.": Marguerite Henry. *A Pictorial Life Story of Misty*. Rand McNally 1976.

the state of Virginia: Corrected Typescript Research Notes. MHC. Box 2 Folder 1.

attendees was 6.5 years old: *Misty Birthday Party Scrapbook*. July 1948. MHC Box 15.

in our pasture with our other horses.": Mary Jon "Jonnie" Edwards Interview August 13, 2021.

unusually nice human : "Marguerite Henry Ad." *Chicago Daily Tribune*, November 11, 1951.

CHAPTER 13: SWIMMING WITH HORSES

If you ever get a chance to swim on horseback, it's one of the coolest things ever. Sometimes there are vacation places where you can rent a horse to ride and the guide will take the riders into water and do just that. I once did that on a ride in Turks and Caicos. I'm pretty sure there are horse rental places in Florida where you can do that too.

CHAPTER 14: MARGUERITE'S WRITING SECRETS

to comb their own curls.": Alberita R. Semrad, "Marguerite Henry, Newbery Medal Winner." *Publishers' Weekly*, March 26, 1949.

share the richest nuggets of their past": Marguerite Henry, "Horse Sense is Stable Thinking," *The Wayne-DuPage Hunt: A Chronicle of Events 1928-1980. Edited by Robert L. Sirotek, The Wayne-DuPage Hunt, 1980.*

but I never did.": Schuman, Ed. *Story of a Book*. Pied Piper Productions, 1980.

CHAPTER 15: NOTES EVERYWHERE

a quick visual outline.": Gertrude B. Jupp, "My Little Sister Marguerite Henry." *Horn Book Magazine*, January-February 1950.

after Marguerite has described them": Wesley Dennis, *Tribute to Marguerite*. MHC Box 29 Folder 4.

CHAPTER 16: THE STRUGGLE TO WRITE WELL

my work was more fun.": Marguerite Henry, Rough Draft of *Something About the Author* MHC Box 2 Folder 11.

you couldn't be happy doing anything else": *Marguerite Henry No. 4*. April 1967. SCPL.

wrote Marguerite back: 1961 speech to the American Library Association, *Who Carry Umbrellas*. MHC Box 22 Folder 11. This transcript of this speech was empowering to me as a writer, and I marveled at how smart it was to reach out to the very best in the field to learn their ways. How much dedication it took to locate the addresses of the writers and type (on a typewriter—and I read somewhere she was not an efficient typist) all the letters and mail them out and then wait for the replies. It must have been a gratifying mail day when she received each response.

dash off to a library": Marguerite Henry, *Dear Marguerite Henry*. Rand McNally & Co., 1969.
caressing the words": Ibid.

CHAPTER 17: RESEARCH AND COZY DETAILS

perfect connotation." Alberita R. Semrad, "Marguerite Henry, Newbery Medal Winner." *Publishers' Weekly*, March 26, 1949.
Independence Rock: Independence Rock Folder. MHC Box 20 Folder 1.
picture a scene as if they were right there": *Letter to Mr. Merrit*, February 25, 1976. MHC Box 27 Folder 10.

CHAPTER 18: TRAVELING TO THE SETTING

the actual writing: *Letter to Mary Alice Jones,* October 20, 1967. MHC Box 16 Folder 15.
the splendors of the ride.": Marguerite Henry, *Something About the Author*. 1988.
know how it would taste": Marguerite Henry, *Dear Marguerite Henry*. Rand McNally & Co., 1969.
like a headless turtle": Ibid.
traveled to Italy three times": *Marguerite Henry Newslet-*

ter No. 5. Leaf Raking Time 1967. SCPL.

fitted neatly into place": Marguerite Henry, *Dear Marguerite Henry*. Rand McNally & Co., 1969

as though I had lived it myself": Marguerite Henry interviewed for Rand McNally by Roy Porter, July 1961.

CHAPTER 19: LIBRARY ADVENTURES

with encouragement and faith": *Untitled Document 3 Reasons Marguerite Loved Libraries*. MHC Box 13 Folder 11.

transported into the past.": *Marguerite Henry Newsletter No. 6*. Spring 1968. SCPL.

poking around in the stacks for more.": Marguerite Henry, *Album of Horses*. Rand McNally, 1951.

to the Lipizzaners in Austria." Ibid.

CHAPTER 20: FAN LETTERS AND SCHOOL PICTURES

foxes and burros, all manner of things.": *Marguerite Henry Newsletter No. 9*. Winter 1969. SCPL.

reply to fan mail on her behalf: *Gertrude Jupp Letter*. 9 Mar. 1968. MHC, Box 23 Folder 13.

she was the real thing.": Bonnie Shields, February 11, 2022.

my way of saying, I love you.": *Marguerite Henry Newsletter No. 9*. Winter 1969. SCPL.

CHAPTER 21: YOUNG FRIENDS

As I type these notes today, May 6, 2024, I just got back from meeting another one of Marguerite's young friends. Roy VanMeter lived in Wayne in the 1940s. He was one of the local children who visited Marguerite's home and met Misty and had birthday cake. In fact, his picture is in *A Pictorial Life Story of Misty*. He's the little boy in a striped shirt, standing fourth from the right. He said riding Misty was a thrill, and somewhere at his house he has a sticker that's a horseshoe with Misty's autograph on it. He won it for a game at the pony party.

CHAPTER 22: INFLUENCE BEFORE INFLUENCERS WERE A THING

Eddie the Elegant Elephant: *Rand McNally Eddie the Elephant at Marshall Fields*. Rand McNally Collection, Box 24 Folder 380.
she has to have a little handout of oats": "Album of Horses Interview." *Feature Foods Program*, Radio Broadcast, WLS, November 12, 1952. MHC Box 28 Folder 1.
enjoy looking them over": Marguerite Henry, *A Pictorial Life Story of Misty*. Rand McNally, 1976.
sugar lumps, apples and cookies.": *Publisher's Weekly*. 30

Aug. 1952, pp. 823–24.

pony birthday party: *16mm Misty Birthday Party.* MHC, Box 28 Folder 3.

brought down the house": Marguerite Henry, "Horse Sense is Stable Thinking," *The Wayne-DuPage Hunt: A Chronicle of Events 1928-1980. Edited by Robert L. Sirotek, The Wayne-DuPage Hunt, 1980.*

ask that the law enforcers uphold it": *Marguerite Henry Newsletter No. 4.* April 1967. SCPL.

has brought a big victory": *Marguerite Henry Newsletter No. 7.* Autumn 1968. SCPL.

wild horse so important to western history": Ibid.

CHAPTER 23: CHINCOTEAGUE PONY FUN FACTS

It all started with Marguerite": Allison Dotzel Interview, July 2, 2022.

map of the U.S. on her withers": *The Dynasty of Misty Note.* MHC Box 15 Folder 12.

CHAPTER 24: PONY PENNING PRELUDE

mare neighing to the colts.": Marguerite Henry, *Dear Marguerite Henry.* Rand McNally & Company, 1969.

CHAPTER 25: FACE TO FACE WITH WILD PONIES

Remember, if you come face to face with a wild Chincoteague Pony, don't try to feed it. However, if you meet a domesticated Chincoteague Pony at someone's horse farm, I bet if you ask the owner, they'd let you feed the pony an apple or carrot.

CHAPTER 26: A WALK ON THE BEACH

I've now been to Assateague Island four times. The beach is beautiful (the water is a little too cold for me), and you can find large, perfect seashells. Here's a fun fact about Chincoteague: many people used crushed shells as their driveway instead of a gravel driveway. Isn't that cool?

CHAPTER 27: CHINCOTEAGUE PONY SUPERFANS

Misty of Chincoteague, **it's a dream of a story":** Cindy Faith led the Chincoteague Step Through Time Tours (I participated in two walking tours) during Pony Penning Week 2022. One tour was of the historic downtown, highlighting the unique past and culture of Chincoteague Island, the other was held at the Beebe Ranch. At the time of this writing, the ranch was just purchased by the Museum of Chincoteague; the museum will keep the history of Misty alive.

CHAPTER 28: GAMES ON HORSEBACK

Miss Kendy owns a wonderful collection of every book that Marguerite Henry ever wrote. She has even written books about the ponies! Her most recent titles are *Run, Pony Run* and *Swim, Pony Swim*. They are for young readers (younger than you—maybe like first grade) and colorfully illustrated by a young woman who used to be a student at the school where Miss Kendy was a librarian. Maybe one day you will write or illustrate books too.

CHAPTER 29: THE PONY SWIM

If you are scratching your head thinking, "Hey, this chapter was a lot like the first chapter." You're right. But the wild pony swim is so cool it's worthy of having two chapters dedicated to it. Are you ready to go watch it yourself one day?

CHAPTER 30: BIDDING ON A FOAL

I determined to meet the author in person." Charles Hillinger. "Introduction," *The Illustrated Marguerite Henry*. Rand McNally & Company, 1980.

CHAPTER 31: THE SWIM HOME

I must confess that Sara in this chapter is actually a woman named Sydney. My editor said it was too confusing to have two Sidneys in the book since Marguerite's husband's name was Sidney, and my new horse crazy friend's name is Sydney. Just thought you should know.

CHAPTER 32: A WEBSITE FOR A PONY

Misty's a pivotal part of my life": Matt DesJardins Interview, August 12, 2022. If you haven't visited MistysHeaven.com, the website Matt started to provide information about Misty and her descendants, take a gander. There are loads of photos, articles and family trees. And the site is continually updated. For example, in late May of 2023, a woman connected with Misty's Heaven and provided photos and background information about Wings, the pony who sired all three of Misty's foals.

CHAPTER 33: A PICTORIAL LIFE STORY OF MISTY

expanded our hearts to fill both": Marguerite Henry, *A Pictorial Life Story of Misty*, 1976.

a tiny light in the surrounding gloom": Fred Rasmussen, "'Misty of Chincoteague' Tale Gallops on Horse: Marguerite Henry, Who Died Recently, Wrote 59 Books, but Her Tale of Two Orphans and a Horse Remains a Breed Apart." *The Baltimore Sun*, December 27, 1997.
hardest thing I have ever done": Ibid.
submitting to smothering hugs": Marguerite Henry, Letter to Sandy Price, August 18, 1986. MHC Box 16 Folder 1.
never, never write at all": Marguerite Henry. "Misty Revisited." *Just About Horses*, Winter 1977.

CHAPTER 34: BOOK IDEAS AND UNPUBLISHED MANUSCRIPTS

scientists call it spontaneous combustion": *Marguerite Henry Newsletter No. 4*. April 1967. SCPL.
am disappointed Marguerite didn't go for it: Georgia Glynn, *Letter to Marguerite Henry*. March 29, 970. MHC Box 23 Folder 12.
a book for another publisher": Bennet Harvey, *Letter to Director of Colonial Williamsburg*. 1962. MHC Box 23.
I. . . keep thinking of him": Marguerite Henry, *Snowman Notes*. MHC Box 4 Folder 9.
get a hold on your heart strings": Mary Alice Jones, *Letter*

to Marguerite Henry. September 15, 1957. MHC Box 16 Folder 15.

CHAPTER 35: MARGUERITE'S TWILIGHT

His ashes were scattered at sea: Dale Leatherman, "Marguerite Henry: Forever Young." *Equus Magazine*, https://equusmagazine.com/horse-world/young021603/.
working on *Brown Sunshine*—and she was HAPPY!": Bonnie Shields Email. January 20, 2023.
memory to enfold it and a heart to love it'": Marguerite Henry, *Something About the Author*. 1988. MHP.
Relating to a horse makes us better people": Marek Oziewicz Interview. September 28, 2022.
"This note washes away all the work": Dina Stallings, *Letter to Marguerite Henry*. November 11, 1980. MHC Box 5.

CHAPTER 36: MARGUERITE'S KINDNESS

decorated with a sketch of a seahorse": Marguerite Henry, *Letter to Mr. and Mrs. Starn*. July 24, 1983. Miss Molly's Inn, Chincoteague Island, Virginia gave me a copy of the letter which they have on hand for guests.
It was too generous of praise": Marguerite Henry, Post-It Note on unpublished *Mini Horses*. 1987. Box MHC Box 15.

13 million copies of her books: Charles Hillinger, "Horse Lovers' 'Dear Abby'" *Los Angeles Times*, November 11, 1979.

all the waiting and longing": *Letter to Marguerite Henry*, 1979 MHC.

CHAPTER 37: GETTING LOST WHILE THE ARTWORK WAS BEING FOUND

I like to be thought of in that way": "Album of Horses Interview." *Feature Foods Program*, Radio Broadcast, WLS, November 12, 1952. MHC Box 28 Folder 1.

popularity is not diminished": Nancy Stenard, *Letter to Marguerite Henry*. January 22, 1995. MHC Box 25 Folder 5.

lively pursuit of word-chasing": Rough Draft of *Something About the Author* MHC Box 2 Folder 11.

one of the hardest things she has ever had to do: Lee Galda Interview August 11, 2022.

Braille books: Norah Smaridge. *Famous Modern Storytellers for Young People*. Dodd, Mead & Company, 1969.

CHAPTER 38: MARGUERITE, MY MUSE

I feel moved to do greater things in my life": Lizabeth Hizey, *Letter to Marguerite Henry*. February 4, 1993. MHC Box 8 Folder 15.

Image Credits

Chapter 1: by Kelly Cosby. See her work at kmconlinegallery.com.

Chapters 2-3: by Carolyn Rikje Photography. See her work at https://carolynrikjephotography.com/

Chapter 4: of Misty and Mary Ellen, photographer unknown.

Chapter 5: by the author while riding Creole Rose at Garner Ranch in Mountain Center, California.

Chapter 6: of Marguerite's Newbery Medal taken by the author while researching the Kerlan Collection of Children's Literature at the University of Minnesota.

Chapter 6: of Misty at the banquet courtesy of Grand Rapids Public Library.

Chapters 7-8: by the author at the Milwaukee County Historical Society in Milwaukee, Wisconsin.

Chapter 9: Engagement photo courtesy of the Wayne Historical Preservation Society.

Chapter 10: courtesy of the DuPage County Historical Museum.

Chapters 11-12: courtesy Kerlan Collection of Children's Literature.

Chapter 13: 1982 photo of the author riding Jim Dandy taken by Cindy, the woman who opened up the world of horses for Susan.

Chapter 14: original art of Misty, Friday and Jiggs frolicking at Mole Meadow by Bonnie Shields, The Tennessee Mule Artist. Bonnie was Marguerite's last illustrator.

Chapter 15: calendar notes image taken by the author while researching the Kerlan Collection of Children's Literature.

Chapter 16: courtesy of the Wayne Historical Preservation Society.

Chapter 17: notes from *Album of Horses* taken by the author while researching the Kerlan Collection of Children's Literature.

Chapter 18: courtesy of the Wayne Historical Preservation Society.

Chapter 19: by Carolyn Rikje Photography.

Chapter 20: photos taken by the author while researching the Kerlan Collection of Children's Literature.

Chapter 21: photos of the bridle rosettes worn by Skippy the Cleveland Police horse featured in *Album of Horses* taken by the author when visiting Ed Richardson.

Chapter 22: taken by the author April 21, 2024 giving her horse Knight a birthday cake based on Marguerite's cake for Misty.

Chapter 22: Spanish Mustangs. Unknown photographer, unknown date, photographic print. Institutional Photograph Collection, Dickinson Research Center, National Cowboy & Western HeritageMuseum. PH1969.008.

Chapter 23: by Kelly Cosby.

Chapter 24: of the Misty statue on Chincoteague Island by Shelley Paulson. See gorgeous photos of horses at www.shelleypaulson.com. She has a stunning portfolio Chincoteague Ponies on her website.

Chapters 25-26: by NWJ Design & Photography www.nwjdesign.com

Chapter 27: Kelly Cosby's photo of Riptide, the famous Chincoteague Pony Stallion who has a private Facebook Group of 3,700 fans.

Chapter 28: by the author during the Chincoteague Pony Drill Team Open House, July 2023.

Chapter 29: by NWJ Design & Photography.

Chapter 30: by Kelly Cosby.

Chapter 31: by NWJ Design & Photography.

Chapter 32: graphic created by Amy Summer Ellison. Check out MistysHeaven.com for more Misty fun facts.

Chapter 33: photos of Miniature Horses found in Marguerite's research folder at the Kerlan Collection of Children's Literature.

Chapter 34: memo photo by the author while researching the Marguerite Henry Collection at the Kerlan Collection of Children's Literature.

Chapter 36: selfie of the author while staying at Miss Molly's Inn on Chincoteague Island, October of 2022.

Chapter 37: photo by the author of the 1951 WLS radio interview album with Wesley Dennis and Marguerite Henry at the Kerlan Collection of Children's Literature.

Chapter 38: courtesy of the DuPage County Historical Museum.

ACKNOWLEDGMENTS

Thank you to the awesome young readers who took the time to give feedback: Grace Troast, Helen Miller and Katherine Jones.

Thank you to editors Sirah Jarocki and Holly Caccamise. I'm grateful to Marlene Friedland, Heidi Walker, Joyce Bloemker, Sarah Hickner and Linda Nelson for additional feedback.

Much love to Carolyn Rikje, Brian Ware, Shelley Paulson, Amy Ellison, Rebekah Hart, Amanda Geci and Kelly Cosby. Thank you to archive experts Lisa Von Drasek, Steve Schaffer, Karen Spillman, Jordan Cloud and Lulu Zilinskas. I couldn't have done this without you.

To the 2023-2024 fourth and fifth graders of Chincoteague Elementary School—I'll always remember our fun time together in September 2023 when I shared about my favorite author. You inspired me to write this book. Thank you!

101 Writing Exercises for the Horse Lover

Unbridled Creativity is a writing and journaling activity book for all horse-loving ages.

AVAILABLE NOW @ saddleseekshorse.shop

About the Author

Susan, a former English and history teacher, shares her equestrian passion on her blog SaddleSeeksHorse.com. She also co-hosts the Barn Banter by Horse Illustrated podcast and writes for horse magazines. When Susan's not writing or speaking about Marguerite and Misty, she's trotting around on her horse Knight in Bull Valley, Illinois. Susan would love to do an author talk at your library, school or club. Send her an email at susan@saddleseekshorse.com or reach out via Instagram or Facebook at @saddleseekshorse.

www.ingramcontent.com/pod-product-compliance
Lightning Source LLC
Chambersburg PA
CBHW060557080526
44585CB00013B/600